Valle Crucis Abbey
Pillar of Eliseg

D. H. Evans BA, FSA

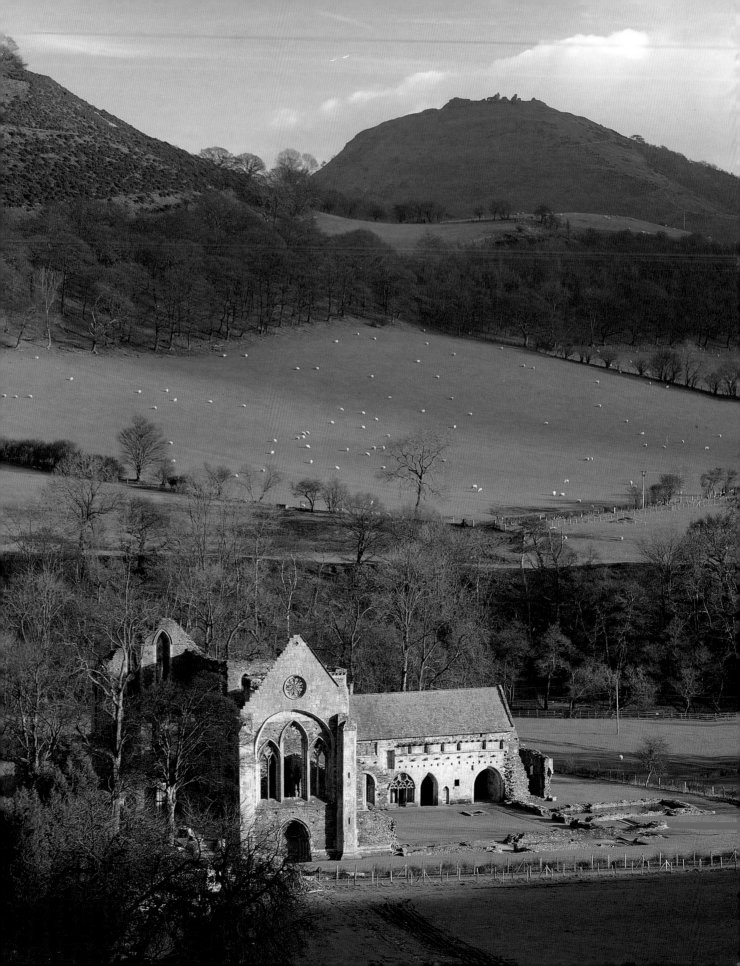

A History of Valle Crucis Abbey

'...Valle Crucis, solemnly seated at the foot of the mountains, on a small meadowy flat, watered by a pretty stream, and shaded with hanging woods.'

Thomas Pennant, *A Tour in Wales*, volume I, (London 1778)

The Cistercian abbey of Valle Crucis lies just a few miles outside the eisteddfod town of Llangollen, at the foot of the steep climb to the aptly named Horseshoe Pass. Its eye-catching ruins sit on the west bank of a fast-flowing little stream that eventually finds its way into the river Dee. In the 1790s, the scene was captured in a magnificent watercolour by the young J. M.W. Turner (1775–1851). The west front of the abbey church is seen nestling in the valley of the Nant Eglwyseg. Beyond lies the striking backdrop of Dinas Brân, crowned with the skeletal remains of its renowned Welsh stronghold.

The abbey's Latin name — meaning 'valley of the cross' — is derived from the Pillar of Eliseg. In fact, the pillar is a ninth-century Christian memorial cross, set up by Concenn of Powys to record the ancestry and ancient glories of his forebears. The remains of the cross-shaft stand on a small hillock, no more than a few hundred yards to the north of the abbey site.

Valle Crucis was founded in 1201 by Madog ap Gruffudd Maelor (d. 1236), ruler of northern Powys (Powys Fadog), and was situated in the commote, or district, of Iâl at the heart of this old Welsh principality. The abbey was colonized by the Cistercians, or white monks, as they were commonly known. The initial community, probably of thirteen monks, came from Strata Marcella, near Welshpool, another Cistercian foundation supported by the princes of Powys. During the Middle Ages, Valle Crucis was sometimes known as *abbatia de Llanegwest*, a name that derives from the Welsh settlement of Llanegwestl which had earlier stood on the site of the abbey.

Occupied by Cistercian monks for more than three hundred years, religious life ceased at the abbey in 1537. Now, nigh on five hundred years later, following the ravages of plunder and decay, the ruinous walls of the abbey still speak eloquently of their austere beginnings and their subsequent decline and abandonment. It is a tale that has to be teased from the weathered masonry and interwoven with what little documentary evidence survives; a tale that explains why men settled here in pursuit of religious devotion and what drove them to leave this most peaceful location.

Opposite: Valle Crucis Abbey with the ruins of Castell Dinas Brân in the distance. Founded by Prince Madog ap Gruffudd Maelor (d. 1236) in 1201, the abbey's isolated and peaceful location at the foot of the Horseshoe Pass was typical of those chosen by the Cistercians — white monks — for their communities.

Left: The abbey's name, Valle Crucis (Latin for 'valley of the cross'), refers to the nearby Pillar of Eliseg, erected in the ninth century by Concenn of Powys to commemorate his ancestors. In this early nineteenth-century engraving of the cross, the buildings of the abbey are visible in the distance (National Library of Wales).

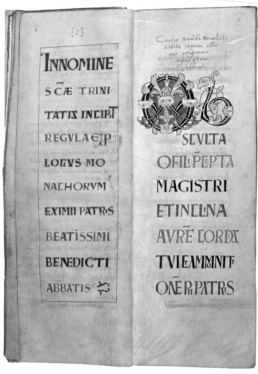

Around A D 540, St Benedict of Nursia set out practical guidelines for the ordering of monastic life around worship, manual labour and study. Later known as the Rule of St Benedict, *this became the most influential template for monastic observance in medieval Europe. This manuscript of the* Rule *was produced around 1100 (© British Library Board, Harley Ms. 5431, ff. 6v–7r).*

Below: The Cistercian order was the most successful of several movements that sought to reform traditional Benedictine monasticism around the beginning of the twelfth century. This thirteenth-century English manuscript illustration portrays the early growth of the order (Cambridge University Library, Ms. Mm.5.31, f. 113r).

The Cistercians and their Way of Life

Monasticism in Europe is almost as old as Christianity itself. One of the earliest and certainly most influential sets of practical rules on how to run a community was drawn up by St Benedict at his monastery of Monte Cassino, Italy, about A D 540. From the early eighth century onwards the *Rule of St Benedict*, as it became known, was increasingly adopted by religious communities all over Europe. These monks, known as Benedictines, devoted their lives to worship, manual labour and study. Each community, or abbey, was ruled by an elected abbot.

Standards of discipline and devotion varied from abbey to abbey, and by the eleventh century they had fallen considerably. The Cistercian order was one of the many movements — and ultimately one of the most successful — which attempted to reform the monastic ideal at large. The order takes its name from

Cîteaux (in Latin *Cistercium*), in Burgundy, eastern France, where an abbey was founded in 1098 by a group of monks searching for a more austere and exacting style of life. In their daily life the Cistercians followed the basic *Rule of St Benedict*, but they added a number of other conditions. Their abbeys were to be sited in remote locations away from other settlements and their buildings and all furnishings were to be plain and unadorned with elaborate decorations. Their clothes were to be woven with undyed wool, which gave rise to them being known as the white monks, and they observed strict rules of silence and diet.

Cistercian abbeys were working communities based upon a series of outlying farms known as granges, often sited near enough to the abbey to be worked daily. The labourers at these granges were known as lay brothers, or *conversi*. Although untutored, they also formed part of the abbey community, but lived under less strict rules than the choir monks (p. 7). They were subject to the authority of the abbey cellarer, who was also responsible for the provision of food and drink.

Unlike the earlier Benedictine abbeys, the Cistercian houses were linked together in a closely bound order, which every year held a meeting of the General Chapter at Cîteaux, at which all Cistercian abbeys were to be represented. New abbeys were founded as colonies, or daughters, of existing houses, and a mutual system of visitation between mother and daughter abbeys ensured that standards were maintained. This, too, guaranteed the success of the order and by 1155 there were no less than 340 Cistercian monasteries throughout Europe.

The Cistercians in Wales

Monasticism in Wales was already flourishing by the sixth century, but its origins and traditions lay somewhat outside of mainstream European developments. In the centuries that followed there was to be little standardization, and variety was almost certainly one of the major characteristics. Thus, the Normans entering Wales at the close of the eleventh century would have found little to resemble the Benedictine foundations in England, or those of their French homeland. Soon, however, the Normans began to found their own religious houses in the newly conquered territories of southern and eastern Wales.

The Cistercian settlement of Wales is often viewed in terms of two distinct streams. The earliest houses, such as Tintern (founded 1131) and Margam (1147), followed the Norman advance and continued to be patronized by Anglo-Norman and Marcher lords throughout their history. In contrast, the second stream flowed through the heartland of Welsh Wales — *pura Wallia* — and was fed by the important

The first Cistercian monastery in Wales, Tintern Abbey, was founded in 1131 by the Anglo-Norman lord of Chepstow (Monmouthshire), William fitz Richard of Clare (d. 1138), in the beautiful Wye valley.

Above: Although Whitland Abbey owed its foundation in 1140 to the Anglo-Norman bishop of St Davids, Bernard (1115–48), it was from here that the Cistercian order spread throughout pura Wallia *— Welsh Wales. Whitland had three daughters in Wales — the abbeys of Strata Florida, Strata Marcella and Cwmhir — and four granddaughters, including Valle Crucis. This counter-seal of Whitland Abbey dates from 1303 and depicts a crozier, a symbol of the abbot's dignity and authority (© British Library Board, Additional Charter 8414).*

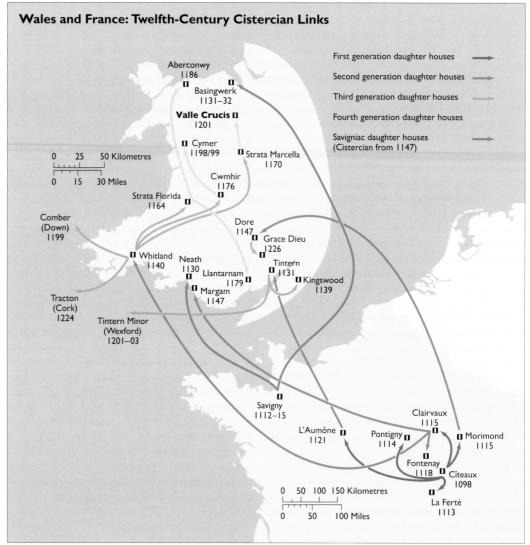

Wales and France: Twelfth-Century Cistercian Links

First generation daughter houses

Second generation daughter houses

Third generation daughter houses

Fourth generation daughter houses

Savigniac daughter houses (Cistercian from 1147)

Aberconwy 1186
Basingwerk 1131–32
Valle Crucis 1201
Cymer 1198/99
Strata Marcella 1170
Cwmhir 1176
Strata Florida 1164
Comber (Down) 1199
Dore 1147
Grace Dieu 1226
Whitland 1140
Neath 1130
Llantarnam 1179
Tintern 1131
Kingswood 1139
Margam 1147
Tracton (Cork) 1224
Tintern Minor (Wexford) 1201–03
Savigny 1112–15
Clairvaux 1115
L'Aumône 1121
Pontigny 1114
Morimond 1115
Fontenay 1118
Cîteaux 1098
La Ferté 1113

0   25   50 Kilometres
0   15   30 Miles

0   50   100   150 Kilometres
0   50   100 Miles

Right: Monks from Whitland colonized Strata Marcella in 1170 at the invitation of the prince of southern Powys (Powys Wenwynwyn), Owain Cyfeiliog (d. 1197). The abbey prospered and by 1201 it could send out some thirteen brothers to become the first members of the new Cistercian community at Valle Crucis. Scarcely any trace of Strata Marcella remains above ground, but earthworks and other features are still visible from the air (Royal Commission on the Ancient and Historical Monuments of Wales).

mother house at Whitland (founded 1140). From this source the order spread among Welsh society, finding far more favour and acceptance than was ever achieved by the older Benedictine houses.

Five further abbeys, including Strata Florida (founded 1164), Strata Marcella (founded 1170) and Valle Crucis itself (founded 1201), were to stem from Whitland and to flourish under the patronage of native Welsh princes. These houses were more overtly Welsh in character: in addition to their close links with the Welsh princes, many of their abbots and monks were Welsh, and they soon became important centres for Welsh learning and literature.

Everyday Life in a Cistercian Abbey

Within a Cistercian monastic community, the choir monks and the lay brothers each led very different lives. A choir monk spent his life in prayer and study, with a limited amount of manual work and a certain degree of literary activity such as copying manuscripts. His day was organized around a long series of services in the abbey church. There were eight main services, each of which was known by the Latin word for the hour at which it was sung or said. The times of these services varied with the season, but a 'typical' day may have begun at 2.00am with the monks rising for Matins. With breaks for simple meals, work and a little rest, the monks would have continued through to the evening service of Compline, finally retiring around 8.00pm.

The lay brothers spent most of their lives in manual labour — except for Sundays and major feast days. They rose at dawn, said the service of Prime in the nave of the church, and then went off to their various places of work. They attended only three meetings a year in the chapter house with the rest of the monks and ate in their own refectory, where they were granted an extra allowance of bread. They slept in their own dormitory, and were also required to keep the rule of silence as far as possible.

As the centuries progressed, the monastic population at any Cistercian house became far more diversified. From a very early date, abbeys would have been obliged to house pilgrims and travellers requiring hospitality, and, from time to time, would have taken in the poor and the sick. By the fourteenth century it was becoming common for certain individuals to spend their retirement within an abbey. These people were called 'corrodians' and included retired abbots and priors, superannuated servants and various laymen who had purchased annuities, together with board and lodging, as a sort of insurance against old age. So in 1530 John Howe paid £20 in return for which he was assigned a chamber containing 'an adequate bed with sheets', and he was to receive 'food and drink daily at dinner and supper and after customary hours'. He was also entitled to have candles for light, his clothes laundered, his hair and beard cut, and one new tunic a year.

The later Middle Ages were also to witness an increasing dependence upon lay servants in the day-to-day life of any Cistercian house. The lay steward, for example, came to play a very important role in the management of abbey estates, particularly after the decline of the lay brotherhood. By this time, too, the evidence from excavations of the south range at the abbey suggests that the community would have enjoyed 'a solid diet of bread, mutton, salt pork and bacon, cheese, eggs and river fish', and that this would probably have been 'much more varied and nutritious than that of ordinary peasant folk in the area'.

The day of a Cistercian choir monk was structured around the opus Dei (the work of God), which consisted of eight choral services, or divine offices, performed in the choir of the abbey church. In the intervals between the offices, Masses would be celebrated at the various altars in the church. This manuscript illustration from 1268 shows monks singing in the choir; above a priest elevates the Host during Mass (Stiftsbibliothek Zwettl, Ms. 400, f. 1v).

Two Cistercian monks splitting a log are shown in this manuscript, completed at Cîteaux in 1111. The Cistercians reasserted the importance of manual work as a component of monastic life, and choir monks were expected to labour in the fields and elsewhere. However, most of the work required to sustain a monastic house and its estates was done by the illiterate conversi, or lay brothers. Although members of the monastic community, for the most part the conversi lived, worked and worshipped separately from the monks (Bibliothèque Municipale, Dijon, Ms. 170, f. 59r).

Like all Cistercian abbeys, Valle Crucis was dedicated to the Blessed Virgin, who is shown holding the infant Christ on this common seal of the house from 1534 (The National Archives: PRO, E 326/10141).

History of the Abbey

Unfortunately, very few monastic documents survive from Valle Crucis. As a result, there are long periods about which little is recorded. The great majority of the many building campaigns that took place here are undocumented; even the great fire, which swept through the monastery in the mid-thirteenth century, is not mentioned in any surviving records. Most of what is known about the abbey's history comes from secondary sources. With the suppression of Valle Crucis in 1537, the quality and volume of surviving documentation increase dramatically, and its post-medieval history is better known.

The Thirteenth and Early Fourteenth Centuries

Although the native Welsh chronicle, *Brut y Tywysogyon* (*Chronicle of the Princes*) records that the abbey was built in 1200, Cistercian documents record that the beginning of monastic life took place on 28 January 1201. The founder was Prince Madog ap Gruffudd Maelor, who ruled northern Powys, an extensive territory stretching from the valley of the Tanat in the south to the outskirts of Chester in the north-east. Throughout much of his life, Madog was an ally of Prince Llywelyn ab Iorwerth (Llywelyn the Great, d. 1240) and safeguarded Gwynedd against a flank attack

by the English. The foundation of his abbey was encouraged by the abbots of Whitland, Strata Marcella, Strata Florida and Cwmhir.

The mother house was Strata Marcella, which had been founded in 1170 and was now in a position to send out some thirteen monks to colonize this new daughter. The date of 1201 marks the arrival of these monks and their occupation of a temporary church and domestic buildings on the site. There had been an earlier settlement at this place, but Cistercian authorities required that abbeys of the order should be located in isolated places away from towns and villages, 'far from the concourse of men'. The foundation of Valle Crucis meant that the inhabitants of Llanegwestl had to be moved. They were transferred to Stansty, located in the founder's lands of Maelor Gymraeg (Bromfield), to the north-east.

Despite the well-laid preparations, all did not go smoothly at the new abbey. Within a year or two of its foundation, complaints were made to the General Chapter of the order that the abbot seldom celebrated Mass and was known to abstain from the altar. In practice this probably meant that he was celebrating Mass less than once a week, perhaps on account of the growing number of priest-monks at this date, who celebrated individually; this change in patterns of worship may also have led to the redesign of the eastern ends of Cistercian churches in order to accommodate more altars. Three decades later,

Before the white monks came to Valle Crucis, seen here in an aerial view from the north-west, a small settlement called Llanegwestl stood on the site. Cistercian legislation specified that the order's abbeys were to be sited in isolated places, 'far from the concourse of men', so the inhabitants were moved to Stansty in Maelor Gymraeg (Bromfield). The memory of the settlement lingered and Valle Crucis was sometimes called abbatia de Llanegwest *(abbey of Llanegwestl) during the Middle Ages (RCAHMW).*

in 1234, the abbot was once more in trouble with the General Chapter, this time for allowing women to enter the precincts of the house. The rule excluding women from entering Cistercian monasteries was enforced strictly, but the abbot's explanation must have been convincing as the General Chapter classified this particular transgression as only a light fault.

The founder and patron, Madog, died in 1236 and was buried in the abbey church as were other members of the royal dynasty of northern Powys in due course. In the same year, his son, Gruffudd Maelor (d. 1269), confirmed the gifts and liberties granted to the abbey by his father. Soon afterwards, although there is no documentary record of it, a disastrous fire must have swept through the monastery. The fire left extensive traces on the earliest masonry of the church and throughout the southern range of domestic buildings (pp. 19, 21). It is possible that the fire was an incident in the wars that troubled Wales at this time. However, given the extensive burning in the south range (the site of the kitchen and possibly the warming house too), it is equally plausible that the fire was accidental and simply swept through the claustral ranges into the church.

Misfortune struck again later in the century when Valle Crucis suffered badly during the two Welsh wars of King Edward I (1272–1307) in 1276–77 and 1282–83. The abbot had been pro-Welsh in his sympathies; indeed, a list of the monks present in 1275 shows that the entire community was Welsh. In the same year, he had been one of seven abbots of Welsh Cistercian houses to write to the pope defending the reputation of the prince of Wales, Llywelyn ap Gruffudd (d. 1282), as a 'protector … of our Order', against charges that had been laid against him by Anian, bishop of St Asaph (1268–93). In the following year, perhaps in gratitude for this support, the prince loaned Abbot Madog (about 1275–84) £40, which enabled him to travel to the papal court at Rome. The abbey's estates became a natural target during the wars and it was one of several houses in north Wales to suffer substantial damage to its property. Indeed, the abbey received compensation twice: first, in December 1283, when the king gave a present of £26 13s. 4d. having perhaps seen the damaged buildings for himself and again, in 1284, as part of a wider round of payments at the end of the

This fragment of a grave slab (now on display in the abbey dormitory) may have formed part of the tomb of Madog ap Gruffudd Maelor (d. 1236), the ruler of northern Powys who was the founder and patron of Valle Crucis. For much of his life he was an ally of the prince of Gwynedd, Llywelyn ab Iorwerth (d. 1240). The fine carving on the slab shows clear parallels with that on the coffin lid in Beaumaris church, which almost certainly came from the tomb of Llywelyn's wife, Princess Joan (d. 1237).

King Edward I (1272–1307) in a marginal drawing from an exchequer roll of 1300–01. The pro-Welsh sympathies of Abbot Madog (about 1275–84) made the estates of Valle Crucis a natural target during Edward I's Welsh wars in 1276–77 and 1282–83. The abbey eventually received two payments from the king, totalling £186 13s. 4d., in compensation for the substantial damage inflicted on its property (The National Archives: PRO, E 368/72).

In this manuscript illustration of 1111, a Cistercian monk is shown wielding an axe against the trunk of a tree. Above him a novice — a prospective monk undergoing a year's probation — uses a billhook to trim the branches. In the early years of the order, the Cistercians were well known for clearing land to bring it under cultivation (Bibliothèque Municipale, Dijon, Ms. 173, f. 41r).

wars. This time, the abbey received £160. It was the highest payment to any of the Welsh Cistercian houses; the next comparable sums were £100 paid to each of the abbeys of Aberconwy and Basingwerk. The estates of all three abbeys lay in the heart of the war zone and much of the damage is likely to have been to stock and crops plundered by Welsh and English armies alike. Perhaps another reason why the Welsh houses were treated so fairly is that the Cistercian order had earlier been prudent enough to contribute £661 towards Edward's campaigns in Wales.

Edward I clearly valued the advice and help of several prominent Welsh Cistercian abbots and in 1294 expressed his 'especial confidence' in the loyalty of the abbot of Valle Crucis, placing him in

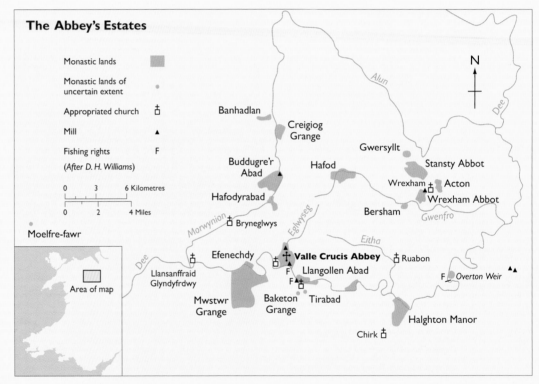

The Abbey's Estates

Monastic lands
Monastic lands of uncertain extent
Appropriated church
Mill
Fishing rights   F
(After D. H. Williams)

0   3   6 Kilometres

0   2   4 Miles

Area of map

Banhadlan
Creigiog Grange
Gwersyllt
Buddugre'r Abad
Hafod
Stansty Abbot
Wrexham   Acton
Wrexham Abbot
Hafodyrabad
Bersham   Gwenfro
Moelfre-fawr
Morwynion   Bryneglwys
Eitha
Efenechdy   Valle Crucis Abbey
Ruabon
Llansanffraid   Llangollen Abad
Glyndyfrdwy   F   Overton Weir
Mwstwr   Baketon   Tirabad
Grange   Grange
Halghton Manor
Chirk
Alun
Dee
Eglwyseg

The Economy of the Abbey

Most Cistercian houses relied heavily upon local patrons for the granting of large tracts of land, with rights of grazing, mining and fishing. This enabled them to build up a thriving mixed economy. Many of the Welsh houses owned extensive tracts of upland, suitable only for sheep grazing and forestry, but this was supplemented by farms known as granges on the more fertile soils, lower down in the valleys. The lay brothers provided a readily available labour force and in these terms Valle Crucis was no different from other abbeys. However, whereas most Welsh Cistercian houses relied heavily upon wool production to provide the bulk of their income, Valle Crucis was to find it from a different source.

Its most profitable lands were grouped around the abbey at Llanegwestl. In addition, it had hill grazing and moorland on the granges of Mwstwr, Hafodyrabad and Buddugre'r Abad, together with arable fields, water meadows, parkland and woodland on the lowland granges of Halghton Manor, Stansty Abbot and Wrexham Abbot. It also had a dairy farm (vaccary) at Nante and from its foundation it held scattered rights of pasture in Maelor Saesneg, Iâl and elsewhere. A system of transhumance was practised, moving livestock up onto the hills for the summer charge of administering the estates of Roger of Mold whilst the latter was serving the Crown in Gascony. In July 1295 Edward again visited Valle Crucis, resulting in 'oblations of the king at the great altar' of two 'cloths'.

We gain some idea of the relative wealth that Valle Crucis had acquired by the end of the century from a papal taxation document known as the *Taxatio Ecclesiastica* of 1291. The Welsh wars certainly appear to have taken their toll on its lands and granges. Valued at a modest £14 14s. 8d., they were among the poorest group of Cistercian estates in Wales. However, with the addition of tithes from appropriated churches, the total assessment was over £91, placing it as the fourth wealthiest Cistercian house in Wales.

months and back down for the winter. This practice was to bring it into dispute with the abbeys of Strata Marcella (1225) and Cwmhir (1227) over neighbouring estates. These upland granges supplied meat, milk products, leather and wool, whilst the lowland granges provided wheat and other crops. The importance of fish in the Cistercian diet, particularly in earlier centuries, is reflected not only in the abbey fishpond, but also in the weir it held at Overton and the fishing rights it enjoyed at Llangollen on the river Dee.

By the mid-thirteenth century wool production had become the major activity at the abbey. However, although this was sufficient to warrant the conversion of the corn mill on the home farm into a fulling mill to process the wool, it never really formed a significant portion of the abbey's income. The real wealth of Valle Crucis lay in grants of tithes from seven neighbouring parishes. Initially granted to help bolster the abbey's income during its formative years, by 1535 the tithes of benefices, including Bryneglwys, Chirk, Llangollen, Llansanffraid Glyndyfrdwy, Ruabon and Wrexham, were providing a staggering 74 per cent of its annual revenue.

In addition to its rural land holdings, the abbey also held two urban manors: Llangollen Abad, with its own mill and fishery, and Wrexham Abbot, which had its own monastic court and mill. Whilst these major assets brought in substantial revenue, the abbey also had almshouses in Llangollen, where they looked after the poor and perhaps in Wrexham too.

The gradual disappearance of the lay brothers during the fourteenth century brought about a number of changes on the abbey's estates. At the home farm they were replaced by a small paid labour force, whereas the bulk of the outlying lands was leased to tenants and the estates were organized into small townships. Another source of income in the fifteenth and sixteenth centuries was

pilgrims, who came to marvel at the speaking statue of the Risen Christ — one of a number of such miraculous statutes, shrines or relics that were claimed to exist at Welsh monasteries. There was also a local tradition that the water from the well by the roadside could 'perform wonderful cures'.

The later Middle Ages saw the increasing tendency to rent out property, including most of the abbey's urban holdings in Wrexham. Overall, by the suppression, Valle Crucis was content to draw rent from whatever property it held. All of this was a far cry from the ideals and austerity of its founding monks.

Valle Crucis had a number of upland granges that provided pasturage for sheep and cattle, and at Nante it had a vaccary, or dairy farm. This early thirteenth-century manuscript illustration shows a milking scene (© British Library Board, Harley Ms. 4751, f. 23).

The arable lands in the abbey's home farm and in its lowland granges produced wheat and other crops. Although some of the work on the home farm may have been done by choir monks, like this reaper shown in a Cîteaux manuscript of 1111, the conversi *shouldered the greatest part of the burden. After the disappearance of the lay brothers in the later fourteenth century, the home farm was worked by paid labour and the outlying granges were leased to tenants (Bibliothèque Municipale, Dijon, Ms. 170, f. 75v).*

By the end of the century, it seems certain that the monks had become thoroughly involved with Welsh literary activity. Primarily, it appears that the continuation of *Brut y Tywysogyon* (*Chronicle of the Princes*) for the years 1282–1332 was compiled at Valle Crucis. The abbey clearly continued to enjoy the patronage of the princes of northern Powys; Madog ap Gruffudd (the great-grandson of the founder of the abbey) was buried here in 1306 (see p. 51), so too was his cousin, Gweirca, who died in 1290 (see p. 50).

Although Valle Crucis experienced difficulties in the aftermath of Edward's campaigns and subsequent Welsh uprisings between 1284 and 1295, the early part of the fourteenth century was a period of relative prosperity. Certainly, major rebuilding of the upper part of the west front of the abbey church took place (p. 21). In this respect, Valle Crucis appears to have been more fortunate than many Welsh Cistercian houses, which were experiencing straightened circumstances, especially during the 1330s and 1340s.

The Later Middle Ages

Then, in 1349, the Black Death struck. This, together with changing social conditions, was one of the factors contributing to the decrease in the number of lay brothers living in the abbey during the later fourteenth century and may in turn have led to modifications in the west range. This was by no means confined to Valle Crucis and was occurring at Cistercian abbeys throughout England and Wales.

Nevertheless, the architectural detail of the east range, and particularly of the chapter house and the book cupboard, suggests that a substantial and ambitious campaign of rebuilding took place around the middle of the fourteenth century (p. 21).

The abbey seems to have suffered badly during the Welsh uprising led by Owain Glyn Dŵr at the beginning of the fifteenth century (1400–10). We learn of this indirectly from a petition of 1419 to the pope by Robert of Lancaster (concurrently abbot of Valle Crucis and bishop of St Asaph), claiming that he 'had repaired the monastery on its destruction by fire'. Although Lancaster's term of office as abbot was extended from 1419 to 1433, his relationship with his monks was clearly not good, as the latter were reminded in papal correspondence that they must obey him. Nor did things improve much with the

next abbot, Richard Mason (1438–48), who is alleged to have overseen a period of neglect.

From the middle of the fifteenth century, however, the abbey enjoyed a modest revival in its fortunes. Three of the abbots who were to hold office between about 1455 and 1527 — Siôn ap Rhisiart (about 1455–61), Dafydd ab Ieuan ab Iorwerth (about 1480–1503) and Siôn Llwyd (about 1503–27) — earned for themselves a considerable reputation as scholars, liberal patrons of the Welsh bards, collectors of Welsh literary manuscripts and builders. As such, they were to give the abbey a greater standing in north-east Wales than it had enjoyed for almost two centuries. Another contributing factor to the upturn in the abbey's fortunes may have been that it enjoyed the patronage of the powerful Stanley family from 1484, when they were granted the lordship of Bromfield and Yale [Iâl].

By this time, however, the Cistercian rules of austerity, plain living and strict diet had long since lapsed. This is also reflected in building conversions and the splendour in which later abbots resided. Indeed, the praise lavished upon abbots Siôn ap Rhisiart and Dafydd ab Ieuan ab Iorwerth by the poets, Guto'r Glyn and Gutun Owain, was probably inspired as much by the many sumptuous banquets and rich hospitality they provided as by their religious devotion. Abbot Siôn Llwyd won similar praise from the early sixteenth-century master poet, Tudur Aled (d. 1526).

Abbots Dafydd ab Ieuan ab Iorwerth and Siôn Llwyd in particular were remarkable men who were to bring the abbey a great deal of stability and prestige from the 1480s to the late 1520s, coinciding with the advent and establishment of the Tudor dynasty. Dafydd ab Ieuan ab Iorwerth was clearly destined for high office and went on to become the deputy reformator of the Cistercian order in England and Wales in 1485, and in the last years of his life he was concurrently bishop of St Asaph (1500–03). Siôn Llwyd rose to prominence as one of the overseers for the compilation of the Welsh pedigree of Henry VII (1485–1509). His connections with the royal court continued; in 1518 he was described as 'the king's chaplain and doctor of both laws'. He was subsequently buried at Valle Crucis, but his tombstone was moved after the suppression of the monasteries and placed outside Llanarmon yn Iâl church.

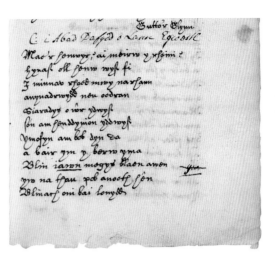

Left: Guto'r Glyn died as a corrodian (p. 7) of the abbey in 1493. He was one of the Welsh bards who lavished praise on Valle Crucis and its hospitable abbots during the monastery's final revival between about 1455 and 1527. In this poem, preserved in a later manuscript, he celebrates the open-handedness of Abbot Dafydd ab Ieuan ab Iorwerth (about 1480–1503) (National Library of Wales, Peniarth Ms. 152B, f. 35).

Sadly, with the appointment of the next abbot, Robert Salusbury (1528–35) the fortunes of the abbey went into an irreversible decline. He was a totally unsuitable candidate, who appears to have been imposed upon the abbey; he was probably under age, never served a proper novitiate as a monk, and does not seem to have been properly professed or elected. A member of a prominent local family, Salusbury appears to have already been implicated in a series of robberies, forcible entries, evictions and assaults, before he was appointed. As such, the new abbot proved so unpopular with the seven remaining monks at Valle Crucis that five of them promptly left for other monasteries. Following a visitation by the abbot of Neath in 1534, the house was placed in the care of the prior. Salusbury was removed to Oxford, but there became a leading personality in a band of robbers and was eventually imprisoned in the Tower of London. The abbey's finances were so bad that the next and last abbot, John Durham, had to borrow £200, just to meet the expenses of his 'induction and installation'.

Not all who entered the monastic life were equal to its rigorous demands, as this fourteenth-century manuscript illustration of a monk suffering in the stocks for his misdemeanours suggests. This was clearly demonstrated at Valle Crucis when Robert Salusbury, a violent and unruly man from a prominent local family, was imposed as abbot in 1528. He controlled the monastery until 1534, when he was finally removed to Oxford. Salusbury was eventually imprisoned in the Tower of London (© British Library Board, Royal Ms. 10 E IV, f. 187).

Above: The illuminated initial on the opening folio of the Valor Ecclesiasticus *depicts King Henry VIII (1509–47) enthroned. The* Valor, *compiled in 1535, surveyed and valued all church property in England and Wales. Valle Crucis was assessed at £188 8s. 0d. (The National Archives: PRO, E 344/22).*

After the suppression of Valle Crucis in January 1537, its fixtures were auctioned. This late medieval chandelier in the parish church at Llandegla and a similar one at Llanarmon yn Iâl may have been amongst the items sold off.

The Suppression and Later History

In 1535 a survey and valuation of all church property in England and Wales, including that of the monasteries, was made for King Henry VIII (1509–47). The results were presented in a document known as the *Valor Ecclesiasticus*, which reveals an assessed income at Valle Crucis of some £188 8s. 0d. — an undervaluation by at least 15 per cent since it excluded several granges and estates. None the less, it was sufficient to rank the abbey as the second richest in Wales. Tintern headed the list with an assessment of £192, though both were small compared with the standard of many English houses.

Following this survey, many of the monastic communities throughout the country must have sensed the forthcoming doom. At Valle Crucis this would have appeared closer when, late in 1535, the king's commissioners visited the abbey. They reported the presence of just six monks. Moreover, the monastery and church were said to be in 'great decay' and the house was some 300 marks (£200) in debt to the king and others.

In March 1536 an act was passed whereby all religious houses with incomes of less than £200 per annum were to be surrendered to the king. Valle Crucis survived probably until autumn 1536, and was finally closed in January 1537. The last abbot, John Durham, received a pension of £23; the few remaining monks were paid wages of £10 13s. 4d. and were dispersed to various surviving Cistercian abbeys.

The abbey's Communion plate was either sold for cash, or sent to London to be melted down. Its fixtures and fittings, everything from chandeliers to bedding, were auctioned on the spot. Some of its bells, for example, found their way into the Shropshire churches of Baschurch and Great Ness, whilst some of its brass chandeliers reputedly hang in nearby parish churches.

The estate was granted in July 1537 to the Yorkshireman, Sir William Pickering (d. 1542), who initially maintained many of the buildings in a weatherproof condition, but was compelled by the terms of his lease to recover as much lead as possible for the Crown. The lead was melted down by workers from Minera, 8 miles (13km) away, using temporary hearths and smelting pits sunk into the cloister; this process continued until 1546. The effect of this lead stripping, together with extensive stone robbing, which began soon afterwards, started the gradual process of decay.

For a short while the Valle Crucis estates were run smoothly, efficiently and profitably. Pickering and his son, however, were absentee landlords and unpopular both with their tenants and with their neighbouring landowners. Soon, rents were withheld, tenancies were disputed and properties were broken into and plundered. The isolated abbey buildings were particularly vulnerable. Between 1542 and 1544 Edward Almer, a neighbouring landowner, systematically raided the abbey for glass, lead and stone for the new mansion that he was building at Pant Iocyn, in Acton township.

The estate passed to another absentee landowner, Sir Edward Wootton (d. 1625), when he married the Pickering heiress in 1575. The early years of his ownership saw large parts of the abbey fall into further ruin, with surrounding inhabitants continuing to rob the finer stone; in 1586 the antiquary, William Camden (d. 1623), described Valle Crucis as 'wholly decayed'.

It was during this period that a resident tenant, Edward Davies of Esclusham, moved into the abbey precinct and it may have been he who converted the east range of the cloister into a dwelling house. Nevertheless, despite Davies living on the premises, the attacks on the abbey continued. One of his neighbours, John Edwards of Chirk, forcibly entered the premises with his servants, seized deeds and other documents belonging to the former abbey (including its foundation charter), and tried to establish his ownership of the property.

In 1606 Wootton renewed his lease of the abbey for another 100 years, and commissioned a new survey and rental of the estate. This shows that at that date the tenant was Richard Matthews, and he was in possession of the site of the abbey 'with the now [new] dwelling house there' — which is presumably the conversion of the former east range of the monastery.

After several further changes of ownership, Valle Crucis eventually became part of the Coed Helen estate. Early eighteenth-century prints and drawings show the abbey roofless and ruinous, but in the second half of that century the chapter house was converted into a farmhouse, and some new buildings were added. Amongst the latter was a cottage at the east end of the abbey church, which incorporated a date-stone inscribed T. Ll 1773 (the initials being those of Thomas Lloyd). Most of the buildings were used as a farm. A large house was built at the south end of the east range, another in the west range, and yet another on the north side of the cloister. The former refectory became a barn, and a dairy was built outside the kitchen.

By this time, however, Valle Crucis had become established as one of the main attractions for tourists and painters in search of the Picturesque in north Wales, including Paul Sandby (d. 1809) and J. M. W. Turner (d. 1851). With the advent of the railway in the 1840s, Llangollen was placed firmly on the tourist route from the English Midlands to Snowdonia, and the abbey began to experience its first contact with mass tourism.

During the mid- to later nineteenth century, archaeological excavations were carried out on the site, and the estate embarked upon a long-term programme of clearance and restoration. In 1872 the services of the great Victorian architect, Sir Gilbert Scott (d. 1878), were retained for the repair of the west front of the church, and in 1896 Sir Theodore Martin (d. 1909) restored the buttresses at the east end; the latter work was completed just in the nick of time, for six weeks later an earthquake was to cause part of the north transept and a dividing wall between its chapels to collapse.

In 1950 the abbey ruins were sold to the then Ministry of Works, which began careful consolidation in the following year. Since that time responsibility has passed to the Ministry's successor, Cadw, the historic environment service of the Welsh Assembly Government.

By the late eighteenth century, Valle Crucis had become a popular destination for tourists and artists in search of the Picturesque. In this oil painting by Paul Sandby (d. 1809), the abbey ruins, seen from the south-east, nestle in the midst of a serene rural landscape. The church stands roofless, but the smoke curling from a chimney and the laundry hung out to dry indicate that the east range of the monastic buildings had been converted to use as farm buildings (National Library of Wales).

Artists and Tourists at the Abbey

As the abbey fell into disuse and ruin, so it became a magnet for artists and tourists alike in search of the Picturesque and the Romantic, especially during the late eighteenth and early nineteenth centuries. Earlier views, however, by Humphrey Llwyd (1584) and the Buck brothers (1742) provide important evidence about the state of the abbey buildings at the time (p. 23).

The Romantic movement and the growth of tourists looking for places of great beauty in north Wales made Valle Crucis a favourite stopping place for travellers passing through the Horseshoe Pass on their way to Snowdonia. One of the first well-known travellers to popularize the abbey and place it firmly on the tourist trail was Thomas Pennant (d. 1798), in volume one of *A Tour in Wales* (1778), illustrated among others by Paul Sandby (d. 1809).

Sir Richard Colt Hoare (d. 1838) visited twice, in 1796 and 1797, and produced two sketches of the ruins which show the west front of the abbey church prior to its restoration by Sir Gilbert Scott in 1872. Colt Hoare summed up the attraction of the place for many artists: 'The remains of the celebrated abbey in Valle Crucis are about 2 miles distant, and though not so well preserved as their beautiful architecture should have merited, still merit the attention of every traveller who will view them as an artist or antiquarian'.

The celebrated artist, J. M. W. Turner (d. 1851), visited the site in 1794 and in 1808. The first visit produced an impressive pencil and watercolour study of the abbey viewed from the west, with Dinas Brân looming large in the background. By the time of his second visit, Turner had become more interested in depicting the landscape setting and the gradations of light upon the scene; his 1808 sketch depicts the ruins from much further away, illuminated by bright sunshine, with the mountains of Eglwyseg set behind in shimmering waves of light.

The period between 1790 and 1820 saw visits from a succession of travellers who featured the abbey in their published tours: Richard Warner (d. 1857) in *A Second Walk through Wales* (1800), William Bingley (d. 1823) in *North Wales* (1804) and Edward Pugh (d. 1813) in *Cambria Depicta: A Tour through North Wales* (1816). Artists continued to visit in the nineteenth century including the celebrated Norwich School artist, John Sell Cotman (d. 1842), George Pickering of Chester (d. 1857) and John Chessell Buckler (d. 1894).

By the mid-nineteenth century, the greater publicity given to the abbey by these paintings and drawings, coupled with the advent of the railways making access so much easier, meant that Valle Crucis was becoming a popular destination for day trips from the English Midlands. Not everyone was to welcome the growth of mass tourism. An anonymous correspondent, writing in 1863, complained that: 'It has become the fashion in summer, not only for visitors of the middle and upper classes to flock hither in great numbers, but very often "excursion trains" from the manufacturing districts [of England] run to Llangollen, and vomit forth their miscellaneous crowds upon the abbey....'

George Borrow, writing in *Wild Wales* in 1862, complained that the access into the abbey was then 'through a farmyard, in which was [an] abundance of dirt and mire'. However, this seems to have been a singular and atypical view of the site and most later Victorian writers seem to have been struck by the picturesque beauty of the abbey ruins, with their lush growth of ivy and magnificent setting.

Above: This mid-thirteenth-century manuscript illustration depicts masons and carpenters building a church. The first structures at Valle Crucis were probably wooden, but work on stone buildings must have begun soon after the first monks arrived in 1201 (Trinity College Library, Ms. 177, f. 60r — The Board of Trinity College, Dublin).

Right: The church at the Burgundian abbey of Fontenay is often cited as a classic example of the Bernardine plan. The east end shows the short, box-like presbytery and transepts with eastern chapels characteristic of the plan (The Art Archive/Dagli Orti).

Bottom right: The remains of the south transept at Basingwerk Abbey (Flintshire). The churches at Valle Crucis and Basingwerk were both relatively modest realizations of the Bernardine plan, but Valle Crucis rose to a greater height and displayed more elaborate architectural detailing.

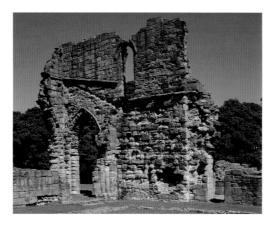

The Development of the Abbey Buildings

As with medieval monastic houses in general, the building history of Valle Crucis was long and varied, with several principal phases of development.

Building Before the Fire

In the absence of more extensive archaeological investigation, we know very little about the temporary buildings, which are assumed to have been erected and occupied by the initial colony of monks arriving from Strata Marcella in 1201. However, it seems likely that both their church and their domestic accommodation were constructed of wood at this time. During excavations in the 1970s, traces of timber buildings were found in the south range and at the southern end of the east range. They show that a certain amount of ground preparation had taken place before any construction commenced, and that timber structures remained in use in parts of the monastery for much of the first half of the thirteenth century.

Following ground preparation, architectural evidence from the surviving church demonstrates that work must have begun almost immediately on the construction of permanent stone buildings. The basic plan of the abbey church certainly dates from the early thirteenth century. It is relatively modest, but faithful to the 'Bernardine' plan, so called after St Bernard of Clairvaux, with a short vaulted presbytery, transepts with two eastern chapels, and a nave of just five bays. Thought to have been based on a set of proportional principles, the Bernardine plan was at its most popular during the second half of the twelfth century and can be found at numerous Cistercian houses across Europe. The main elements comprised a comparatively short, box-like presbytery, transepts with low eastern chapels and an aisled nave. Although the church at Valle Crucis was a modest example of this plan, it was still a substantial structure and rose to a greater height than Basingwerk Abbey and had more elaborate piers and richer architectural details.

By 1225 the eastern half of this church was well advanced and work had already started on building the stone roof over the presbytery, the transepts and the crossing. By about 1240, the western half of the church had also been laid out and work had started on the lower parts of the walls and the piers, which separated the nave from its north and south aisles. It seems, too, that this western area was meant to have had a stone roof.

Meanwhile, as construction of the church was progressing, work had started on the domestic buildings around the other three sides of the cloister. By the middle of the thirteenth century it is likely that the western and southern ranges had been completed in stone. In addition, it is presumed that the eastern range would have been in a similar state of completeness by this time. This eastern range was much modified in later centuries with only the sacristy at its northern end surviving from the initial layout. What is more, it appears from excavation that in the thirteenth century this range extended up to 40 feet (12m) farther south than the later arrangement might suggest.

With building having reached this stage, a disastrous fire evidently swept through the monastery. We have no documentary evidence for this, but it is clear that extensive alterations were made to the original scheme in the later thirteenth century, particularly in the church. During the fire, the roof — such as existed — no doubt collapsed and burning timbers fell against the walls of the church. In places, the dressed stonework in these walls is now stained to rose red. The fire also left considerable traces in the southern range of the cloister.

Rebuilding and Changes in the Later Middle Ages

Rebuilding work began in the mid-thirteenth century and within the abbey church it is possible to identify the distinction between the masonry existing before the fire and that built after this date. The earlier work, in the lower courses of the walls, is of roughly faced rubble, incorporating many large irregular boulders. The later work is also of rubble construction, but it consists mainly of small flat slates instead of large boulders.

In the main, the reconstruction of the church involved the heightening and completion of the east end, including its upper windows and external buttresses, the south transept, most of the nave and the west front with its main central doorway. The fire also clearly damaged the crossing tower and much of its west side had to be extensively rebuilt. Further

While the abbey church was under construction in the first half of the thirteenth century, work also proceeded on building the domestic ranges around the cloister; all three were probably complete by the middle of the century. Much of the east range was extensively remodelled in later centuries, but the sacristy, with its elaborate round-headed doorway, survives from the initial layout.

Firefighters are shown struggling to save a monastic church in this manuscript illustration from 1190–1200. Around the middle of the thirteenth century, a major fire caused extensive damage at Valle Crucis and led to significant alterations to the original scheme, particularly in the still unfinished church (© British Library Board, Additional Ms. 39943, f. 31v).

The Cistercian Plan

Cistercian abbeys were built to a remarkably uniform plan reflecting the centralized organization of the order, and in this Valle Crucis proved no exception.

The most important building was the church, generally planned in the shape of a cross and orientated east–west. Here, as in other Cistercian houses, the presence of two distinct communities meant the church was virtually divided in two. The eastern half (the presbytery, crossing, north and south transepts) was chiefly the domain of the choir monks, whereas the western half (the nave) was reserved for the use of the lay brethren.

The domestic buildings of the monastery (those in which the monks ate, slept and conducted administration) were arranged around an open square or cloister situated on the south side of the abbey church. To the east of this cloister lay the chapter house, a latrine block and the monks' dormitory on the first floor. The range to the south included the monks' refectory, the kitchen and probably a warming house. On the west side of the cloister, the third range provided dining and sleeping accommodation for the lay brothers.

In addition to these three main ranges of domestic buildings, a passage through the southern end of the east block probably gave access to a secondary cloister housing the monastic infirmary. This was intended for the sick and aged members

of the community who could no longer manage the rigours of the full Cistercian life. Consequently, it tended to be located in the most secluded part of the entire abbey precinct. Although the exact location of the infirmary at Valle Crucis is not known, a document of 1528 indicates that it was still in use.

During the early history of Valle Crucis, this eastern area may also have housed the abbot's house, though, as we shall see, in later centuries he took up residence in the former monks' dormitory. Nothing of the buildings in this area now remains above ground.

The final element in a medieval Cistercian abbey plan comprised those buildings providing facilities for guest accommodation and the exploitation of outlying estates. These could have included a gatehouse, a gatehouse chapel, guesthouse, barns, granaries, stables, a brewhouse, bakehouse, dovecote, mill, dairy and so on (perhaps even a smithy). Many of these were generally located in an area to the west of the church and cloister known as the outer court or enclosure. Once again, at Valle Crucis, although some of these may have been located on the estates themselves, nothing now remains above ground at the abbey site.

The entire complex of conventual buildings would have been set within a much larger precinct. In many houses this would have been enclosed by a stone wall; however, at Valle Crucis, no trace of a medieval precinct wall has been identified, and one of the surviving field names, 'lwyn-y-palys', may indicate that at least part of the boundary was formed by an earth rampart topped by a timber palisade.

The essential features of the Cistercian monastic plan can be traced in this early eighteenth-century bird's-eye view of the French abbey of Clairvaux (Aube). Seen from the south, the monastic buildings are set within a precinct defined by an encircling wall [1]. The cruciform, or cross-shaped, church — easily identifiable with its tall spire in the centre — is orientated east–west [2]. Lying directly to the south of the church's long nave is the open cloister around which the three main domestic ranges are disposed [3]. The infirmary buildings stand south-east of the church [4], while accommodation for guests and various service buildings occupy the western end of the precinct [5] (Bibliothèque Nationale de France, Paris).

ARCHICŒNOBII
CLARÆVALLENSIS
ad Meridiem
PROSPECTUS.
Tab. 3ª

Left: Much of the abbey church, seen here from the north-west corner of the nave, had to be reconstructed in the wake of a devastating mid-thirteenth-century fire. Further work, including a certain amount of refurbishment and ornamentation, took place in the early fourteenth century.

Above: The graceful mouchette, or 'curving dagger', patterns in the tracery of the book cupboard in the eastern cloister range. Architectural details like this suggest that a mid-fourteenth-century date is most likely for the rebuilding of the range.

work on the church was undertaken during the earlier fourteenth century, when the upper part of the west front was rebuilt, as revealed by the inscription which dates the work to the time of Abbot Adam, around 1330–44 (p. 26). Finds of unstratified early fourteenth-century floor tiles in parts of the west range and in the church indicate that a certain amount of refurbishment and ornamentation was also being carried out during this period.

On purely architectural grounds, a date around the middle of the fourteenth century is most likely for a major rebuilding of the eastern cloister range and, in particular, for the chapter house (with its wave mouldings and flowing window tracery) and the book cupboard (with the mouchette, or 'curving dagger', patterns in its tracery), though some authors have suggested this work might be that referred to in Abbot Robert's petition of 1419. It should, however, be recalled that most of the major building campaigns which took place at the abbey are either

undocumented or are very poorly documented, and the rebuilding of the east range is no exception.

The 1970 archaeological excavations have demonstrated that parts of the southern and western ranges were severely damaged in an early fifteenth-century fire, and it seems reasonable to attribute the rebuilding of these two ranges to Abbot Robert, who took up his office in 1409.

Overall, the new east range was to retain the standard Cistercian plan with a square chapter house and a long undivided dormitory on the first floor.

The passage to the south of the chapter house is, however, a little unusual in that it provides a rather more elaborate entry into the eastern part of the precinct than in most other Cistercian abbeys. Although the arch at the far end of the passage is reused, perhaps from the thirteenth-century chapter house, it may reflect a growing tendency amongst the abbots to display their wealth and self-importance. At this date the abbot's house

South of the chapter house, this elegant arch gives access to a relatively elaborate passage through the eastern range. At the time of its construction, this probably provided an imposing approach to the abbot's house in the monastery's eastern precinct.

probably lay beyond this passage to the east of the eastern range itself, and he may well have wanted a more imposing approach to it.

In addition to this major rebuilding work in the cloister ranges, the abbey church was to receive further modification in the late fourteenth or early fifteenth century. In the main, a parapet was added around the church and the east range of the cloister. This was supported upon a series of projecting stone brackets, known as corbels, some of which still survive on the outside faces of the presbytery and the south transept. In addition, within the church itself, the position of the monks' choir was moved further east. The pulpitum, a stone screen wall that physically separated the choir from the nave, was reconstructed under the western archway of the crossing. At the same time, a similar screen wall was built across the east end of the north aisle. The construction of these walls may indicate significant developments in the monastic life at Valle Crucis, with only the east end of the church remaining in regular use. Indeed, the lay brothers had long since ceased to be part of the community and with their disappearance, the nave in a Cistercian church lost much of its original purpose. The resiting of the pulpitum and the addition of a blocking wall at the east end of the north aisle look like an attempt to cut off the eastern part of the church from the remainder, a process which can be traced in a

number of other monastic churches during this period. Further work was carried out during the fifteenth century within the upper walls of the church and finds of window glass outside the north aisle also suggest that many of the windows were reglazed.

From the surviving remains, it appears that the last major rebuilding work at Valle Crucis during the monastic centuries took place on the upper floor of the eastern cloister range. The northern half of this floor was converted into a grand set of apartments for the abbot, with a hall in the former dormitory and a private chamber, known as a *camera*, built over the east end of the sacristy. The southern half of this upper floor was probably converted to provide accommodation for the abbot's important guests.

This change in the use of the east range was revolutionary, and indicates a relaxation in the Cistercian way of life with the abbot living in comparative splendour in the middle of the monastic buildings. These conversions can probably be attributed to two abbots, Dafydd ab Ieuan ab Iorwerth and Siôn Llwyd, who held office between 1480 and about 1527 (p. 13). The poet, Gutun Owain, praised their generosity and spoke of Dafydd as a builder. One of his poems even mentions the exquisite fretted ceiling of the abbot's house, leaving little room for doubt that this was one of the buildings for which Abbot Dafydd was responsible. Gutun also praised the choir of the abbey church,

Below: The wall tops at the junction of the presbytery and the south transept still preserve the corbels that were inserted when the church and the eastern cloister range were crowned with a parapet in the late fourteenth or early fifteenth century.

Below right: A window head in Plas Newydd, Llangollen, filled with fragments of late medieval stained glass collected from Valle Crucis. Such glass suggests that many of the abbey's windows were reglazed in the fifteenth century (Courtesy of Denbighshire Heritage Service).

THE WEST VIEW OF VALLE CRUCIS ABBY, IN THE COUNTY OF DENBIGH.

which he said, with characteristic bardic exaggeration, surpassed even that of Salisbury Cathedral. His verse contains frequent mention of carvings of foliage and statues, and his particular attention to the choir may be a further indication of the concentration of services in the east end of the church by this time.

Post-Suppression Building

Following the suppression of the abbey in 1537, the east range of the former monastic buildings was converted into a dwelling house. The precise date of this conversion is difficult to determine, but it was probably during the last quarter of the sixteenth, or very early in the seventeenth century. An engraving by Humphrey Llwyd (d. 1568), published posthumously in 1584, shows the east range without a roof. The architectural details of the doors and windows in the new dwelling suggest a date of about 1600 for the secular adaptation, most likely during the tenancy of Edward Davies (pp. 14–15).

The principal changes that took place included the rebuilding of the wall tops in the late medieval abbot's hall and the construction of an attic over the former abbot's chamber. In addition, a new gallery,

with a sloping roof, was built on to the east side of the earlier hall. The dwelling probably continued to be occupied in this form until about 1651 when the estate was sequestrated (seized) by Parliamentary Commissioners. An engraving of 1742, by the Buck brothers, shows the building once again without a roof. Finally, during the later eighteenth century, some of the abbey buildings were brought once more into some form of productive use, when much of the site was converted to a farm.

Above: In this 1742 engraving by Samuel and Nathaniel Buck all of the abbey's buildings stand empty and roofless, including the eastern cloister range, which had been converted into a domestic dwelling around 1600 (National Library of Wales).

Left: By the time of this early nineteenth-century drawing, a farm had been established in the abbey ruins and the roofs over the buildings of the eastern range had been reinstated. The smoking chimney served the farmhouse that occupied the monastic chapter house (National Library of Wales).

A Tour of Valle Crucis Abbey

The suggested tour route in this guide begins at the west front of the abbey church, but the various parts of the abbey complex can be visited in any order using the bird's-eye view at the front of the guidebook and the ground plan on the inside back cover. From the church the tour progresses into the nave, or the lay brothers' section of the building. It goes on to examine the monks' choir and presbytery at the east end of the church. The route leaves the building via the north transept to look at the exterior details of the east end. Returning into the church, the tour proceeds to the north and south transepts, before passing through the doorway in the south aisle, out into the cloister.

The tour of the domestic buildings around the cloister begins with the east range, looking first at the sacristy, followed by the chapter house, and eventually proceeding to the monks' dormitory and abbot's apartments on the first floor. The east range ends with the monks' latrine, and from here the tour goes on to examine the remains of the southern range with its refectory and kitchen. Finally, it looks at the west range and the details of the lay brothers' quarters.

The visitor centre is reached via a gentle paved ramp. From here, a gently sloping gravel path leads to the abbey ruins. The grounds are laid to grass.

Above: A floor tile from Valle Crucis bearing the design of a man looking into a mirror, perhaps an allegorical figure representing pride or vanity. Similar tiles have been found at the Cistercian abbeys of Strata Florida and Strata Marcella (National Museum of Wales).

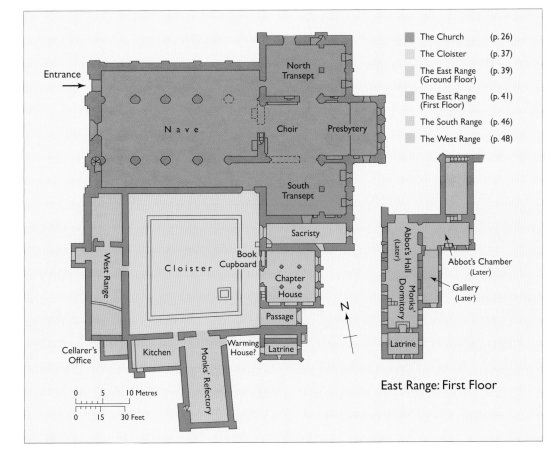

Entrance

North Transept

Nave

Choir

Presbytery

South Transept

Sacristy

Book Cupboard

Cloister

Chapter House

West Range

Passage

Cellarer's Office

Kitchen

Warming House?

Latrine

Monks' Refectory

	The Church	(p. 26)
	The Cloister	(p. 37)
	The East Range (Ground Floor)	(p. 39)
	The East Range (First Floor)	(p. 41)
	The South Range	(p. 46)
	The West Range	(p. 48)

Abbot's Hall (Later)

Monks' Dormitory

Abbot's Chamber (Later)

Gallery (Later)

Latrine

Latrine

N

East Range: First Floor

0   5   10 Metres

0   15   30 Feet

Opposite: The imposing west front of the abbey church at Valle Crucis has survived fire, despoliation and even an earthquake. Today it is the first sight that greets visitors to the abbey.

Entrance

The Church

As in most Cistercian abbeys, the monastic church is built in the shape of a cross. It has a projecting square end known as a presbytery, where the high altar is located. The presbytery is flanked on either side by a transept, each of which has two chapels to the east. A low central tower once stood above the crossing, the area used as the choir, but this has now collapsed. The western half of the church consists of a nave of five bays (that is the space between each pair of pillars), with an aisle on either side. The only pieces of decorated early stonework are the capitals, or the tops of the pillars and columns, and these display a good range of masonry styles typical of the Welsh borders during the early and mid-thirteenth century. Overall, the architecture is fairly plain and relies for its effect on good proportions, simple lines and bold details.

The West Front

The first sight that greets you is the majestic west front of the abbey church. The base of the wall is faced with a fine dressed freestone plinth and there are projecting buttresses along the front and at the corners. These were all built before the great fire and probably date towards the end of the period 1225–40. The elaborate central doorway, on the other hand, was inserted into this wall after the fire, and dates from the mid-thirteenth century. The arch itself is beautifully carved with a variety of 'dog-tooth' ornament.

The main part of the wall is dominated by the great west window, which is also of mid- to later thirteenth-century date. It was originally made up of six main openings, known as lights, which were arranged in pairs. The head of each pair is capped with a small, cusped opening.

The whole window is enclosed within a single arch, the top of which was damaged when the gable of this wall was rebuilt in the mid-fourteenth century. This repair work is faced with large square blocks of dressed stone and its principal feature is a fine central rose window, divided by delicate tracery into eight lights. Above this window is a Latin inscription in Lombardic lettering. This is not very easy to make out as the last two words have been carved on the upper line, but it reads:

**ADAM ABBAS FECIT HOC OPUS
IN PACE QUIESCAT AMEN**

**Abbot Adam carried out this work;
may he rest in peace. Amen**

This was probably Abbot Adam who held office between about 1330 and 1344, since the style of architecture is consistent with these dates. At the very top of the gable is a small square quatrefoil opening, which would have let light into the roof space above the nave.

The modern entrance to the church is through a small doorway, which is medieval in origin and leads into the north aisle of the nave.

Above: The elaborate central doorway in the west front was not routinely used by the monastic community, but functioned as a ceremonial entrance to the church during liturgical processions. The arch is decorated with finely executed 'dog-tooth' ornament.

Right: The delicate eight-light rose window in the western gable of the church is surmounted by a Latin inscription in Lombardic lettering that records that 'Abbot Adam carried out this work'. This points to the reconstruction of the gable during Adam's tenure as abbot between about 1330 and 1344, and the style of the architecture is consistent with those dates.

The Nave

Once inside the church, look back at the internal face of the west front; the view is almost as striking as from outside. Note that where the gable was rebuilt in the fourteenth century, it is much thinner than the rest of the wall and is set back from it [1]. Note too, a doorway [2] leading to a small spiral staircase, which survives to the left (south) of the main west door. It is framed by an arch, which shows signs of wear and has probably been reused from elsewhere in the abbey. The staircase led up to the roof and was probably designed to allow access for maintenance to the space over the nave aisles, which were originally intended to be vaulted in stone.

Turning to the details of the nave interior, we are now in the lay brothers' section of the church. They probably entered the building from their domestic range

through a now blocked doorway at the far west end of the south aisle [3]; the precise position of this doorway can no longer be seen as the outer walls of this part of the aisle have been largely rebuilt (see p. 49). During services the lay brothers are likely to have sat in choir stalls, which were arranged in tiers and backed against the piers at either side of the central nave, thereby blocking off much of the north and south aisles behind (see reconstruction drawing on p. 29).

The nave itself is divided into five bays marked by the bases of five pairs of piers, all but one in their original positions. The lowest parts of the aisle walls are original and date from the early thirteenth century. The best-preserved portions of this early work survive in the north aisle, where you can see a series of small vaulting shafts on the outer wall. These were intended to support a stone roof over the aisle, but this seems never to have been completed. The shafts originally

The western end of the nave of the abbey church — the numbers refer to features discussed in the text. The nave was the section of the church reserved for the lay brothers. During services they would have sat in choir stalls backing against the piers that separated the nave from its two flanking aisles. The bases of all but one of the nave piers survive.

Above: A series of truncated vaulting shafts runs along the north aisle wall. The most easterly rises almost to the level of the stringcourse, while those to the west are shorter. These early thirteenth-century shafts show that the original plan had been to vault the aisle in stone. The change in the character of the masonry above the shafts suggests that the mid-thirteenth-century fire led to the abandonment of that plan. The numbers refer to features discussed in the text.

The eastern end of the south nave aisle. The solid blocking wall (to the left) was constructed in the last bay of the nave to give greater support to the crossing tower in the wake of the fire. The arch at the end of the aisle, which leads into the south transept, was rebuilt at the same time and a pointed relieving arch was inserted above it.

rose from a low bench, most of which has been removed, though some slight remains can be seen as the larger pieces of stone at the bases of the shafts. The most easterly (right) shaft [1] survives almost to the height of the stringcourse, which is the projecting band of masonry running below the windows [2]: the shafts to the west of this stop at a lower level [3]. The masonry above and below this line is different (see p. 19). This must represent a change in plan after the fire. The outer walls may still have been just a few feet high when the decision was taken to roof the aisles in timber rather than in stone. At the eastern end of the north aisle a doorway originally gave access into the north transept (see p. 33). When this was first exposed in 1851, 'traces of a piscine or holy-water stoup' were discovered on the south side of this doorway; unfortunately, the excavators' workmen subsequently demolished all trace of this short piece of walling and the remains of the piscina by mistake. The whole doorway has been reset, and the walling now adjoining this entrance was reconstructed in the later nineteenth century.

Crossing the nave to the south aisle, you should note that its outer walls have been largely rebuilt and this can be seen in the difference between the large blocks of stone used in the lower part of the wall and the later, thinner stone above. Note also the solid blocking wall that cuts off the most easterly bay from the centre of the nave. This was constructed as a somewhat desperate measure after the mid-thirteenth-century fire. At the same time, the archway at the end of this aisle, leading through to the south transept, was rebuilt to provide a strong junction for further alterations going on in the central crossing tower. A pointed relieving arch, to take the weight of the new masonry, can be seen above the archway, as well as three pairs of 'putlog holes' (the rectangular holes that supported the timber scaffolding used by the medieval builders). Also at the eastern end of this aisle is the processional doorway leading into the abbey church from the cloister to the south.

Returning to the centre of the nave, it is important for us to appreciate that during the early Middle Ages the lay brothers' portion of the church terminated at a solid screen wall that was known as the pulpitum, set between the fourth pair of piers. In front of this screen wall would have stood their altar. At this time, the last (fifth) bay of the nave formed part of the monks' choir, which was situated on the other side

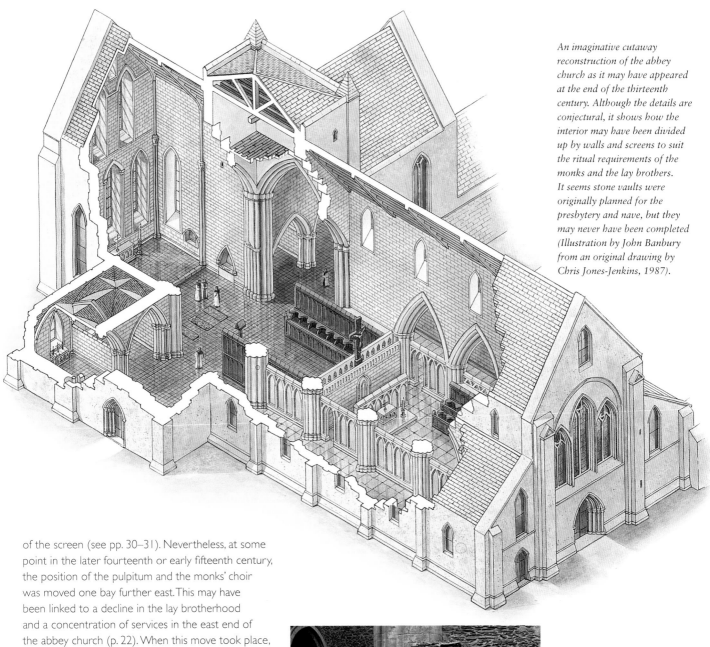

An imaginative cutaway reconstruction of the abbey church as it may have appeared at the end of the thirteenth century. Although the details are conjectural, it shows how the interior may have been divided up by walls and screens to suit the ritual requirements of the monks and the lay brothers. It seems stone vaults were originally planned for the presbytery and nave, but they may never have been completed (Illustration by John Banbury from an original drawing by Chris Jones-Jenkins, 1987).

of the screen (see pp. 30–31). Nevertheless, at some point in the later fourteenth or early fifteenth century, the position of the pulpitum and the monks' choir was moved one bay further east. This may have been linked to a decline in the lay brotherhood and a concentration of services in the east end of the abbey church (p. 22). When this move took place, two altars were set against the west side of the screen in the now lengthened nave. You will notice that only the southern half of the screen and its adjacent altar are now visible. Before leaving the nave, if you look up above the area of solid walling that blocks off the most easterly bay of the south aisle, one side of a window can be seen showing that there must have been an upper, or clerestory, level in this part of the church. When complete, this would probably have consisted of a row of windows set above the line of the aisle roofs.

The remains of the pulpitum in its late medieval position. The pulpitum was a solid stone screen that separated the monks' choir from the nave. The staircase led to a loft that may have housed an organ. The base of an altar survives on the nave side of the pulpitum.

Above: The ornate corbel on the south-eastern crossing pier carried the weight of one of the crossing arches.

Right: The monks' choir and presbytery. A small lancet once filled the apex of the gable and completed the elegant arrangement of the east end windows.

This lead figure of a dove, which retains traces of gilding and perhaps dates from the fifteenth century, may have hung above the pulpitum or a rood beam in the abbey church. It was found at the abbey in 1851 (National Museum of Wales).

The Monks' Choir and Presbytery ◆3

The monks' choir and presbytery can virtually be regarded as a separate church, set within the abbey church as a whole. Cut off by screen walls from the nave and the north and south transepts, it was the scene of all principal services. The monks sat in their choir stalls, arranged in tiers, beneath the central crossing tower. These stalls backed against the screen walls either side and, initially, extended into the last bay of the nave. The monks' high altar was situated in the presbytery at the east end of the church.

Many of the details are best observed from the crossing, between the four great piers designed to support the central tower. This tower was built in the early thirteenth century as part of the original plan, but must have been seriously weakened by the great fire, which followed soon afterwards. The two eastern piers apparently survived this catastrophe and still

represent original work. In contrast, much of the south face of the north-western pier, together with the entire south-western pier, had to be completely rebuilt in the mid-thirteenth century. As noted above (p. 28), it was at this time, too, that the most easterly arch of the south nave arcade was blocked to support the new south-western pier of the tower. No trace of the arch is now visible. The monks' choir stalls would have backed onto this blocking wall at this time.

Observing the details of the crossing itself, note the coarse detail of the later work in the western piers. The best-preserved pier, however, is that at the south-eastern corner, which still stands to its full height. Some 13 feet (3.9m) above the floor level, an ornate stone bracket, or corbel, took the weight of one of the arches that carried the tower over the crossing. The other piers and arches of the tower are moulded with bold, prominent details, particularly on the capitals.

Looking back towards the nave, we have observed that the lay brothers' church was separated from the monks' choir by a screen wall known as the pulpitum.

Only the base of the southern half of this screen survives between the western piers of the crossing. The northern half has presumably been destroyed since the suppression. The surviving fragment contains a staircase, which once led up to a loft. Such lofts often housed an organ in Cistercian churches and medieval Welsh poets writing about Valle Crucis spoke of organ music here. Of particular note, however, is the doorway at the foot of this staircase, which has early thirteenth-century mouldings at its base. This evidence indicates that the entire screen was moved here from its original position between the final pair of piers in the nave.

Following the movement of the pulpitum, the back row of choir stalls would have been built against its east face, looking towards the crossing and presbytery. A similar arrangement then existed on either side of the choir. The screen wall beneath the northern arch of the crossing can still be seen, including its projecting base for the choir stalls. The corresponding wall beneath the southern arch has been removed.

Moving into the presbytery, note that the high altar was situated on a raised plinth at the east end. The presbytery itself is two bays long, and originally it was intended to roof it in stone. Several of the vaulting shafts, which were to bear the weight of this roof, can still be seen in the corners of the east end and in the centre of the north and south walls.

Looking towards the east end, all of the windows at ground-floor level, together with the lower parts of the walls, date from the early thirteenth century. The central lancet window in the end wall was initially taller than those either side, but the whole of its top part was rebuilt after the fire in the mid-thirteenth century, thus making them all about the same height. It has richly moulded sides and carved capitals, unlike the other windows at this level in the presbytery, which are much plainer and without capitals.

All of the upper parts of the walls date from after the fire and belong to the mid-thirteenth century. The upper windows in the east end are fairly plain; they are narrower and more pointed than those beneath. This wall was originally capped with a small upper lancet window, set centrally in the top of the wall, but only its base now remains.

A number of other features of note can be seen in the south wall of the presbytery. To the left there is a double cupboard, known as an aumbry. It contains two small recesses in which the Communion vessels would have been kept. To the right of this there is an arched tomb set in the wall, but this is a Victorian reconstruction using ancient materials. There is a small lancet window high up on this same wall, which originally lit a staircase within the thickness of the presbytery wall. Finally, turning to the north wall of the presbytery, you will notice the remains of an elaborate thirteenth-century tomb. It consists of a small arcaded recess, which had five pointed arches set in front of a chest.

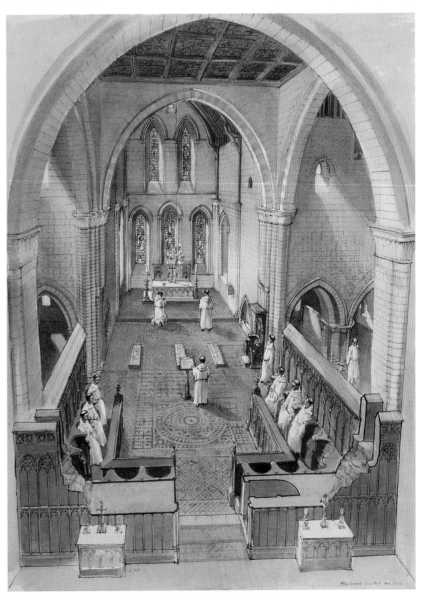

An artist's reconstruction of the eastern end of the church as it may have looked in the early sixteenth century. The pulpitum in the foreground has been cut away to reveal the monks' choir. In the presbytery, two monks kneel at the step that led up to the high altar. The details of the tiling and the wooden ceiling and furnishings are conjectural (Illustration by Terry Ball, 1987).

Entrance

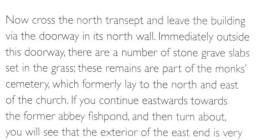

Flat pilaster buttresses are used to striking effect to frame and emphasize the elements of the abbey church's splendid eastern façade.

The Exterior of the East End ◆₄

Now cross the north transept and leave the building via the doorway in its north wall. Immediately outside this doorway, there are a number of stone grave slabs set in the grass; these remains are part of the monks' cemetery, which formerly lay to the north and east of the church. If you continue eastwards towards the former abbey fishpond, and then turn about, you will see that the exterior of the east end is very well preserved. Its bays and angles are strikingly emphasized by a series of flat buttresses, known as pilasters. The only early thirteenth-century examples, which are now fully visible, are to the left, on the exterior of the south transept. These were mostly

built of rubble and had dressed stone only on their corners (known as quoins). All of the other buttresses are almost entirely faced with dressed stone and date from the mid-thirteenth-century rebuilding, as do the upper parts of the walls. All of the windows on the ground floor are tall slender lancets with pointed heads, and were built in the early thirteenth century.

One of the most striking aspects is the way in which the corner buttresses formed two sides of a giant arch that encased the entire east front; the two central buttresses continue up the wall to form a heavy frame around the upper windows.

The whole of this east front was restored in 1896 to save it from collapse. The works entailed a certain amount of rebuilding and the stepped bases of some of the buttresses date from this restoration.

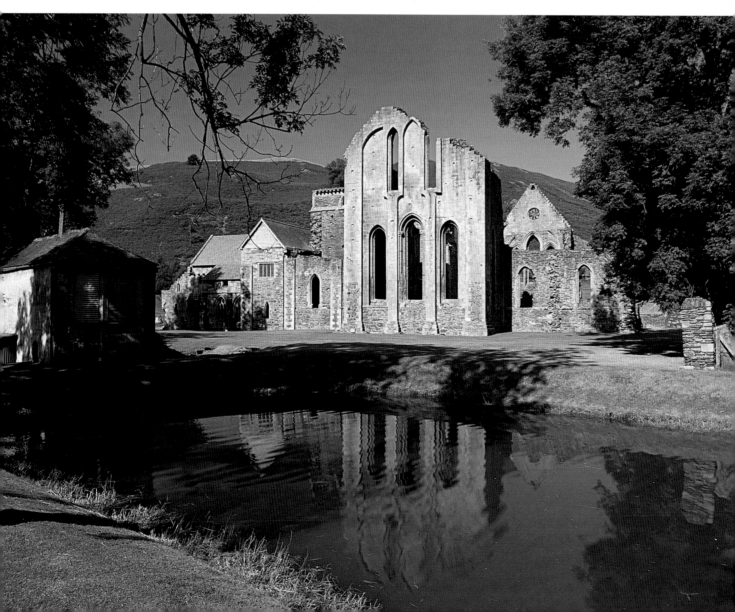

Before retracing our steps to the north transept, it is worth noting the abbey fishpond. This is now the only surviving monastic fishpond in Wales, although most monasteries that did not have nearby fishing rights would originally have had one or more such ponds.

Further evidence for the monks' cemetery can still be seen in the form of grave slabs outside the east wall of the south transept and the chapter house. This group of five graves was uncovered during clearances in the 1880s, and are in their correct positions, although the upright stones around their sides are Victorian reconstructions. Others lie nearby.

The North Transept

Retrace your route to the interior of the north transept. All the surviving parts of this transept date from the early thirteenth century. The upper parts of the walls are likely to have been rebuilt after the fire, but they have long since fallen.

The transept could have been entered from three different directions: the doorway through which we have just returned, from the crossing and from the north aisle of the nave. Initially, the intention was to cover the main body of the transept in stone, but there is no evidence that this was ever completed and it may always have been vaulted with timber.

In contrast, at the east end of the transept, there were two chapels that were covered with stone vaults. Each chapel was lit by a narrow lancet window, situated in the east wall over the altar. In the south wall of the southern chapel are two small cupboards, or aumbries, in which the Communion vessels would have been kept. Next to these is a projecting carved stone basin (or piscina), in which these vessels would have been washed. A second, adjacent piscina is said to have been mounted on a pillar, though no evidence of this now survives on site. The stonework of one of the aumbries and of the south pier of the crossing is heavily burnt to an almost rose red colour, and this is a particularly good place to see evidence of the mid-thirteenth-century fire (see p. 19).

In the north wall of the transept, next to the northern chapel, a spiral staircase led up to the space above both chapel roofs and so into the central tower and on to the roof. It was probably intended to help with routine maintenance.

In the south wall of the transept, which was rebuilt in the later Middle Ages, there is a large medieval tomb recess, but a smaller niche within it is likely to be a Victorian addition.

The large carved stone coffin of plain slab construction was found during clearance in 1851, but is not in its original position.

The curves of the stone vaults that covered the north transept chapels can still be traced on their walls. In each chapel, an altar base survives directly beneath the eastward-facing lancet window. Some of the stone in the southern wall (to the right) has turned an almost rose red colour as a result of the mid-thirteenth-century fire.

Right: The south transept seen from the crossing. The first-floor doorway in the south wall leads from the monks' dormitory in the east cloister range. From here, the night stairs allowed the monks to descend and enter the church directly for the night offices, as shown in the imaginative reconstruction below (Illustration by Chris Jones-Jenkins, 1987).

The South Transept

The south transept is undoubtedly the best-preserved part of the church. The stonework in the base of its walls dates from the early thirteenth century, but all of the upper levels, including the arches and windows of the two eastern chapels, belong to the mid-thirteenth-century rebuilding.

Looking at the south wall, a door with a perfectly plain pointed arch leads to the sacristy. Immediately to the left of this, a small cupboard is recessed into the wall. Further to the right, about 10 feet (3m) above the present ground level, is a wide, richly moulded, early thirteenth-century doorway. This would have been approached by a flight of stairs, probably of wood, giving access to the monks' dormitory on the first floor of the eastern range of domestic buildings beyond. These were known as the night stairs, and were used by the choir monks to attend services in the abbey church during hours of darkness. Above the doorway itself, the top of the south wall contains the bases of three lancet windows set in a single large arch, which formerly rose into the gable.

The west wall of the transept is lit by a single large lancet window, which was modified during the fifteenth century by the insertion of elaborate tracery in its head. Finally, turning to the east wall, the upper level above the archways into the chapels was lit by two small lancet windows. These were, of course, situated above the lean-to roofs of the chapels beyond.

Each of the chapels was lit by a narrow lancet window set in the east wall above the altar. They both had stone-vaulted ceilings and the supports for these post-date the fire. These stone-vaulted ceilings were in turn covered with a sloping lean-to roof and, at a later date, this sloping roof was raised. The result of this was the creation of a small room between the top of the vault and the outer roof. This could be reached from the first floor of the east range of domestic buildings, which lay to the immediate south. A staircase in the thickness of the south wall of the presbytery led up from this room into the main roof space over the eastern end of the church. Looking up

from the southern chapel, towards the southern presbytery wall, it is possible to see the doorway that led to this staircase. From this position, it is also possible to see the line of the sloping lean-to roof that covered the stone-vaulted ceilings.

Altar bases can still be seen in both chapels, but that in the northern (left) chapel is the best preserved. Its front and sides were originally decorated with a line of arches known as blind arcading, but only the base now survives. Some idea of the quality of the blind arcading can be seen in a piece of masonry reset nearby. In the south wall of the southern chapel, a double piscina is set into a recess with a three-pointed, or trefoil, arch. In this case, the priest would have used one of the basins to wash his hands, and the other would have been used for rinsing the vessels. To the right, a fourteenth-century tomb is recessed into the same wall. This recess is covered with a pointed arch, which is decorated with fine foliage detail, but the actual grave slab has disappeared.

Above: The south transept chapels retain much of their stone-vaulted ceilings intact. Two altar bases survive; that in the northern chapel was decorated with blind arcading, the quality of which can be seen on a masonry block reset nearby.

Left: This artist's impression of the two chapels suggests how they might have looked in the late fourteenth century. At each altar, a priest-monk privately celebrates Mass — a practice that became increasingly common in the later Middle Ages as more monks were ordained as priests and therefore obliged to offer Mass daily (Illustration by Chris Jones-Jenkins, 1987).

The Cloister

We can go on to look at the monks' domestic buildings situated around the remaining three sides of the open cloister. On leaving the church, however, you may care to examine the fine detail of the doorway leading out from the south aisle. It dates from the early thirteenth century, and its arch and jambs are richly moulded. The capitals below the arch are decorated with stiff-leaf foliage.

The cloister is a large open space, which is not quite a rectangle. Each side originally had a covered alley, or walkway, with a lean-to roof. These walkways served a far more important purpose than just connecting the various buildings. The alley next to the church, for example, was a recognized place for monks to spend their time studying and reading. The cloister itself was usually kept under grass, but it was sometimes used for more practical purposes, such as a herb garden. At Valle Crucis a walled rectangular basin was set into the south-eastern corner. This must mark the position of the washing trough, or lavatory, at which the monks would have washed before going into meals in their refectory in the south range. No traces of the superstructure remain. During the late 1890s two other large stone-lined troughs were uncovered to the west of this lavatory and probably formed part of the monastic water supply system — one of them perhaps serving the kitchen.

Immediately following the suppression of the abbey in 1537, temporary hearths were built in the cloister for melting lead as the monastic buildings were systematically stripped of any valuable materials. During the later eighteenth century a cart shed and barn were built on the north side of the cloister, adjoining the exterior wall of the south aisle.

The lean-to roofs over each cloister alley were supported against the surrounding ranges and sloped down to an open arcade on the cloister edge. The line of this inner arcade is now marked out on the ground, and architectural fragments uncovered in the 1890s suggest that it was rebuilt in the later fourteenth or early fifteenth century.

A number of significant features can be identified in the wall face of the east range. To begin with, it is possible to pick out the inner line of the sloping roof, which covered the cloister walkway during the later

Opposite: During the day, the monks would usually have entered the church through this magnificent early thirteenth-century processional doorway situated in the north alley of the cloister. Beautifully carved stiff-leaf capitals (above left) support its arch.

Left: The cloister alley adjacent to the church was recognized as the place for monks to study and read. In this thirteenth-century manuscript illustration, St Bernard of Clairvaux (d. 1153) writes, inspired by the hand of God, while two younger monks read at his feet (Bodleian Library, Oxford, Ms. Laud Misc. 385, f. 41v).

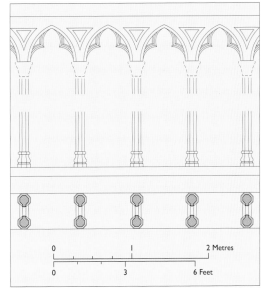

| 0 | | 1 | | 2 Metres |
| 0 | | 3 | | 6 Feet |

The lean-to roofs of the cloister alleys sloped down to an arcade surrounding the open cloister garth (see reconstruction drawing, p. 41). The arcade was probably rebuilt in the later fourteenth or early fifteenth century, and fragments recovered in excavations form the basis for this reconstruction (after H. Hughes, 1895).

Entrance

fourteenth or early fifteenth century. It is clearly marked by the projecting strip of masonry, known as a stringcourse [1], directly beneath the row of first-floor dormitory windows. The main timbers of this roof were supported by the lower line of projecting stone corbels [2] and tied back into the small square beam holes beneath them [3]. This line of corbels has been continued along the walls of the church, where they have been inserted into the earlier stonework.

Looking to the north (left) of this east range, you will see that the level of the earlier thirteenth-century cloister roof was higher. This is marked by the upper row of stone corbels running along the south transept [4], and continuing around to the south aisle of the church, where the corbels have been cut back flush with the masonry. We must be careful not to confuse this with the upper row of corbels on the main body of the east range [5], that which runs above the top of the small dormitory windows [6]. These in fact mark the base of a projecting parapet on which the eaves of the dormitory roof rested, and a corresponding row of corbels can be seen on the other (east) face of this range.

During the fifteenth century, a large part of the upper floor in this eastern range was converted into an elaborate set of apartments for the abbot. The entrance to these apartments was through a doorway, leading from the east cloister walk. If you look up to the top right of the archway into the sacristy, a blocked rectangular opening [7] reveals the approximate position of this doorway (better seen from inside, where it becomes apparent that the present opening is that of a sixteenth-century door which replaced a smaller fifteenth-century doorway in the same position). This was probably approached by a timber stairway and its completion must have involved the demolition of at least a part of the east cloister walk. Indeed, the door would have cut right through the inner line of the lean-to roof.

The upper floor was further modified as a dwelling house in the sixteenth century and the blocked doorway we now see from outside represents alterations made at this time. The new door was made at a slightly lower level and reused part of the fifteenth-century stone arch. It has elaborately moulded sides, which are capped by a horizontal head. This, too, must have been approached by a timber stairway. At the same time, a large rectangular window with four openings, or lights, was inserted into the wall to the immediate left of this door [8].

Seen from across the cloister, the architectural elements of the eastern range of buildings disclose a long and complex building history, stretching from its original construction in the thirteenth century to its adaptation as a dwelling house around 1600. The rubble masonry of the church's south transept and the area around the sacristy contrasts sharply with the later ashlar facing of the rest of the range. The numbers refer to features discussed in the text.

The East Range

The east range comprises by far the best-preserved parts of the abbey. Most of the surviving buildings date from the fourteenth century and later, but excavation has shown that these replaced an earlier range on the same alignment, which extended for at least another 40 feet (12m) to the south. The sacristy at the north, where we begin our tour, is the most obvious survival of this earlier range, but portions of earlier walling seem to be incorporated in parts of the passage and the monks' latrine. The construction of a house in the later eighteenth century has destroyed most of the foundations to the south of the latrine.

The Sacristy ◆7

This room lies immediately south of the south transept; it extends to the full width of the transept and its chapels. The sacristy was where the church vessels and robes were stored, but it also may have served as the abbey book store in the early thirteenth century when it was first built. The room is covered with a long rounded stone roof, known as a barrel vault. The entrance from the cloister is through an elaborate, round-headed doorway, with ornate capitals. It could also be approached from a doorway in the south transept. The room was originally lit by a narrow lancet window in the far wall; there is also a small square-headed window set obliquely in the south wall. At some stage during the Middle Ages there was an entrance into the chapter house in the west end of the south wall, but this has subsequently been blocked. The flagged stone floor in the sacristy probably dates to the use of the site as a farm from the later eighteenth century onwards.

Book Cupboard ◆8

To the south of the sacristy doorway, a richly decorated screen fronts a narrow chamber within the thickness of the west wall of the chapter house. It has its own entrance from the cloister walk, with a large window set on either side, and a fine stone-vaulted roof. The tracery above is ornamented with crude roundels,

shields, and scrolls, and the rough outline of a face. The room may have been used to house the abbey's library. Indeed, at least two books from the library at Valle Crucis are known to survive. One is a fifteenth-century copy of the *Dialogues of St Gregory* (now at Eton College) and the other is a thirteenth-century anthology (now at the Bodleian Library, Oxford), which contains some biblical commentaries of Stephen Langton, a *Life of St Bernard of Clairvaux* and a version of the *Voyage of St Brendan*.

The Chapter House ◆7

The next room to the south is the chapter house, second only to the church in importance in a medieval monastic house. It is a square room, which probably dates mostly from around the middle of the fourteenth century. The exception is the early thirteenth-century north wall, which it shares with the sacristy.

It was here that the monks would assemble each morning to hear a chapter of their *Rule* (hence the name of the chapter house), confess their faults, and receive punishments. Visiting abbots and bishops would hold their inquiries here and it was also the room in which the abbey's dealings with lay landowners and businessmen were likely to have been conducted. Originally, there would have been benches for the monks around the walls, but no trace of these now survives.

Above: The first page of a thirteenth-century anthology of religious works that was part of the library at Valle Crucis. The later medieval inscription in red at the top of the page leaves no doubt about the book's ownership: 'Liber S[an]c[t]e Marie de Valle Crucis' (A book [of the abbey] of Saint Mary of Valle Crucis) (Bodleian Library, Oxford, Ms. e Mus. 3, p. 1).

Left: The book cupboard, a narrow vaulted chamber built into the thickness of the west wall of the chapter house, probably housed the abbey's library. It could be entered from the cloister through this elaborately carved stone screen, or directly from the chapter house.

Above: The chapter house at Valle Crucis is covered with elaborate ribbed vaults that spring from four elegantly moulded piers. The quality of its architecture no doubt reflects the central significance of the chapter house in the life of the monastery. Each morning the monks would gather here to listen to a chapter read from the Rule of St Benedict, to confess their faults and to consider matters affecting the community.

Right: An imaginative reconstruction of one of the daily meetings in the chapter house in the later Middle Ages. The monks listen while one of their number reads a chapter of the Rule *(Illustration by Chris Jones-Jenkins, 1987).*

The chapter house is entered from the cloister through a central doorway, which has a plain pointed arch of two orders, both of which have wave-moulded sections. Indeed, wave moulding is used throughout the room on the piers and vault ribs. Inside, all of the walls, except the north, are faced with dressed stone. Four evenly spaced pillars help to carry the weight of the stone vault and divide the room into three bays in each direction. These pillars do not have any capitals and the stone vaulting ribs rise directly from them, and from the wall face. Together these form an elaborate roof construction, known as 'quadripartite', in which each bay is divided into four compartments.

Three windows, with intricate net-like tracery, are set into the east wall. The central one is a late Victorian reproduction. The original was destroyed in the process of knocking a doorway through the wall, when the building was used as part of the farm.

In many medieval monasteries the chapter house was also a favourite place for burying abbots and other senior clerics. A possible indication of this practice at Valle Crucis is provided by the presence of three large arched recesses in the south wall of this room, which may have contained tombs set on raised ledges. In the later eighteenth or early nineteenth century, when this building was modified into a farmhouse, one of these recesses was entirely rebuilt with new stones, and a fireplace and chimney were inserted. A fragment of a medieval gravestone has been built into the central bay of this south wall.

Turning left out of the chapter house, a small pointed doorway opens on to a staircase in the thickness of the wall. This is the only remaining access to the monks' dormitory on the first floor of this range.

The Monks' Dormitory ◆ 10

In the early Middle Ages, the whole of the first floor of this eastern range was occupied by the dormitory of the choir monks. Initially, it was approached by two separate stairways. The monks attended services at night via the night stairs, which opened from the north of the room and led down into the south transept. Services in daylight hours were attended using the day stairs, which probably led down from the southern end of the range, but the exact position has not been traced.

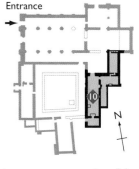

A cutaway reconstruction of the east cloister range as it may have appeared in the mid-fourteenth century. The monks' dormitory occupied the entire first floor of the range. Early Cistercian dormitories were large, open rooms with the monks' beds ranged in two opposing rows. However, in the later Middle Ages calls for greater privacy led to the introduction of individual cubicles, and the room is shown partitioned in this way. The form of the cloister arcade is largely speculative (Illustration by Chris Jones-Jenkins, 1987; with amendments, 2006).

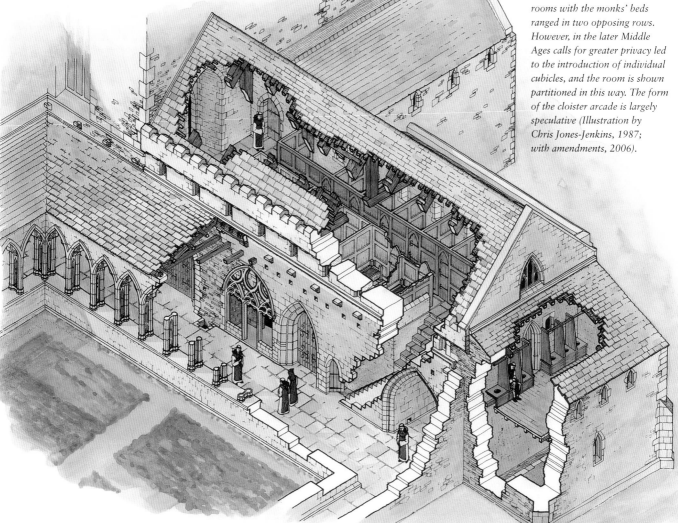

*Below: The interior of the
monks' dormitory. The door and
the window in the far, southern,
wall opened into the monks'
latrine. The narrow windows
in the western wall, which still
display grooves to accommodate
glazing, would have looked
out over the lean-to roof of
the cloister alley below. The
now-blocked doorway in the
foreground was created when the
northern half of the dormitory
was transformed into the abbot's
hall in the later fifteenth century.*

Although the walls date largely from the mid-
fourteenth-century rebuilding, the room has been
substantially altered during the late medieval and
post-medieval periods. It was converted first into
a set of private apartments for the abbot, and later
into a post-suppression dwelling house. It is probably
easier to look at each phase of its development in
turn. We should note at the outset, however, that
the present roofline dates from about 1600 and
represents a rebuilding of the medieval roof.

The Dormitory

During the second half of the fourteenth and the
fifteenth century, the room in which you now stand
consisted of a single long chamber that extended
over the top of the sacristy, the chapter house and
the passage. The monks' cot-like beds would have

been arranged along either wall in typical dormitory
fashion, with a passage down the centre. Even before
the later alterations, demands for greater privacy
may have led to these being divided by partitions
into two rows of cubicles.

The northern end of the room is the southern
wall of the south transept, but all of the other walls
are faced internally with dressed stone. The door
in the north wall dates from the early thirteenth
century and led to the night stairs. Each of the small
narrow windows on the cloister side has a three-
pointed head with narrow grooves down either
side to accommodate glazing. A similar row of
windows once existed in the east wall, but only
three examples at its southern end now remain.

In the south wall, a plain doorway with a
decorated window above, led into the monks' latrine.
To the east (left) of this, a small window also opened
into the latrine; the base of this window is formed
from a reused decorated medieval grave slab.

The Abbot's Hall and Chamber

In the later fifteenth century, the northern half of
the room was converted into a grand hall for the
abbot. The southern end was probably converted
into several apartments for the abbot's important
guests. By this time, the few remaining choir monks
could have found lodgings in a number of other
places within the monastic complex.

A new external door was built into the west wall
at this level and this would have opened on to a
wooden staircase leading down into the cloister. All
that remains of this doorway is the inner face of its
arch; the rest of it was destroyed by the building of
the sixteenth-century entrance in the same position.
Immediately opposite this doorway a large fireplace
was built into the east wall of the former dormitory.

In the far north-east corner of the room, a
doorway opens into a small rectangular room which
served as the abbot's private chamber. The surviving
doorway is late sixteenth century in date, but is
likely to have replaced a smaller fifteenth-century
door. The room would certainly have been heated,
but the existing fireplace dates from the sixteenth
century. Looking above this, the original fireplace is
probably that which can be seen reset in what was
a sixteenth-century attic over this room. It has a small
chimney with moulded stone sides and hood, and
is similar to the large fireplace we have seen in the

*Right: This fireplace was inserted
in the east dormitory wall to heat
the abbot's hall during the late
fifteenth-century conversion.*

An imaginative cutaway reconstruction of the east range in the early sixteenth century when the northern part of the dormitory had been converted into a grand hall for the abbot. The room to the east is shown as his private chamber and the southern part of the dormitory has been divided into apartments for important guests. Although the arrangements shown here are speculative, the construction of the wooden stairs may have led to the removal of the cloister arcade (Illustration by Chris Jones-Jenkins, 1987; with amendments, 2006).

hall. Its original circular chimney can still be seen outside the building, set on a tiny gable.

The south wall of the room is clearly earlier than the remainder, as it incorporates three narrow windows dating to about 1300. This suggests that there may have been a room in this position before the fifteenth-century conversion. It may have served as the lodging of the prior, whose duty it was to see that good order was kept in the dormitory. Another possible explanation is that it was connected with the construction of the small chamber over the roof of the south transept chapels. The two rooms were connected by a door in the north wall of this chamber, leading to a small flight of steps. Although it is not now possible to get into the room over the transept chapels, the doorway affords a good view of the late medieval parapet built on the top of the church walls.

The Late Sixteenth-Century House

Following the suppression of the abbey, these apartments must have presented the cheapest and most convenient alternative for conversion to a dwelling house. In order to understand the alterations carried out at this time, you should first return to the main dormitory range.

The walls of what had become the abbot's hall were rebuilt to support a new roof. Many sculptured fragments were reused in the course of this work, including several door and window jambs. The line of this rebuilding can be easily identified all around the room. As we have seen, a new external door was built in the west wall, reusing part of the stone arch of the fifteenth-century doorway in this position. A large rectangular window was inserted to the north (right) of this door. In the opposite wall, further south, a new fireplace was built, but this is now blocked and partly destroyed.

This room, which opens off the north-east corner of the monks' dormitory, served as the abbot's private chamber during the last decades of monastic life at Valle Crucis. After the suppression, it was further altered when the range was converted into a house around 1600. The large rectangular window in the far (eastern) wall may have been inserted at that time.

The post-suppression alterations included the insertion of this crudely fashioned fireplace to replace a smaller late medieval one. The chimney breast has been cut from an ornate thirteenth-century grave slab. The old fireplace was probably reset directly above its old location in a newly created attic.

The doorway through to the former abbot's private chamber was now replaced with a rectangular door frame. Within the room, possibly at this time, and certainly during the post-medieval period, a large rectangular window was inserted into the east (far) wall. This has now been replaced by a modern copy. The old fireplace was taken out and a larger one built in its place. The new structure is crudely made and a thirteenth-century grave slab was reused as its chimney breast (see p. 50). The old fireplace is probably that reset above in the new attic.

To the right of the fireplace, an opening leads into a new gallery constructed at this time. It was lit by two windows in its east wall and a square-headed mullioned window in its southern wall. Some older fourteenth-century stones were reused in the latter. The west wall is, of course, formed by what had been the external face of the monks' dormitory, and you will notice part of the stringcourse that ran beneath the first-floor windows.

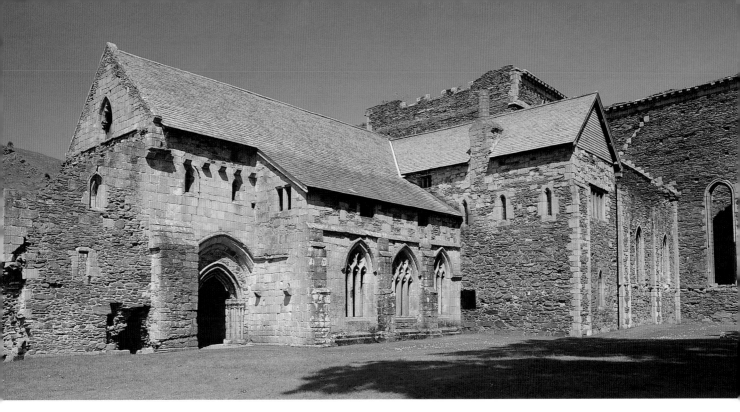

The Passage

Back in the cloister, the next feature to the south is a stone-roofed passage, leading through the east range, probably to the monks' infirmary and possibly to the early medieval abbot's house. The roof of the passage is similar to that of the chapter house, but consists of two compartments, rather than four; here, the central vaulting shafts spring from two fine projecting stone corbels, carved with a male and a female head. At the far end of the passage there is a thirteenth-century arch with elaborately decorated capitals. This is not in its primary position, but has been taken from elsewhere in the abbey and reused. The size of this arch suggests that it could have been used as the thirteenth-century entrance to the chapter house. A small square light on the south side of the passage is probably not original.

The Monks' Latrine

The southern end of the east range now terminates with the monks' latrine, which served their dormitory on the first floor, but excavations have shown that the range extended further south in the thirteenth century. The latrine was a two-storied building and the ground floor had a wooden ceiling. The latrines themselves, situated above, would have emptied through a chute into the stone-lined drain that runs along the north wall of the building. A clear view of this fine drain can be gained from the eastern side of the building, whilst much of the interior of the latrine block can be viewed from the west, where most of the walling has been robbed or has collapsed during the post-medieval period.

The walling in this block seems to be of two periods. Much of the east (far) wall and the surviving sections of the other walls are built of rubble. The upper part of the east wall, however, is faced with dressed stone and probably belongs to the mid-fourteenth-century rebuilding. Thus, it seems likely that the rubble sections may, in part, represent earlier walls. The narrow pointed window set into the south wall is also probably of fourteenth-century date. Higher up the same wall, immediately below the eaves, there are indications at sill level of up to three similar windows, and another example, with a three-pointed head, is set at the same height in the east wall.

The medieval roofline of this building was considerably higher than the present one and it is possible that the level of this roof was lowered when that over the rest of the east range was raised, about 1600. At some stage a small square opening has been cut through the south end wall, just above the level of the plinth.

The eastern façade of the east cloister range. At the southern end, to the left, a passage through the range leads from the cloister to the eastern part of the monastic precinct — the site of the infirmary and probably the abbot's lodgings for some time during the Middle Ages. A fine thirteenth-century arch, perhaps the original entrance to the chapter house, has been reused at the eastern end of the passage.

The single-storey buildings that made up the south range at Valle Crucis only survive as foundations. The large rectangular building, at right angles to the range, was the monks' refectory, and the remains of the kitchen stand to its right. Excavations have revealed that a small room once stood to the left of the refectory; this may have been a warming house.

Entrance

The South Range

The southern range of the cloister comprised a single-storied block of buildings, which included the monks' refectory and kitchen. Much of the site of the south range formerly consisted of boggy ground and, before any construction could take place, this was reclaimed by covering the dampest areas with a raft of brushwood and halved tree trunks. Most of the walls that can now be seen date from the mid-thirteenth century or later, but archaeological excavations have shown that work on the construction of the south range began in the early years of the monastery and that buildings within the range continued in use throughout the Middle Ages. Evidence for two extensive programmes of reconstruction was found. Fire seriously damaged the buildings in the mid-thirteenth century and in the early fifteenth century. In the eighteenth and nineteenth centuries the walls here were much modified when they were incorporated into farm buildings.

The Warming House

The end nearest to the east range is now fronted by a stone wall, which is 3 feet (1m) high and runs along the south side of the cloister walk. This wall dates from the later medieval period, but excavation has shown that it replaced a small room that would have been entered from the cloister (no trace of this room is now visible). It was built in the early thirteenth century and occupies the position where a warming house is usually found in a Cistercian abbey. This was the only place, apart from the infirmary, where a fire was allowed and, during winter months, would have offered welcome relief after hours of prayer and study in the cold and draughty church and cloisters.

However, no hearth or fireplace was found in the room; so, if this was the warming house, it must have been heated with portable braziers. Alternatively, the room may have housed the day stairs: a wooden staircase leading up to the thirteenth-century east range dormitory. In which case, when the east range was rebuilt, the stair would have had to be resited because of the position of the new latrine block.

Excavation established that there were at least two periods of construction and occupation of this room, before it passed out of use, possibly in the later fourteenth or fifteenth century.

The Monks' Refectory ⑭

The monks' refectory, or dining hall, is a long rectangular room set at right angles to the cloister. Its walls still survive to a height of 3 feet (1m) and are built of thinly coursed stone in which larger stones have been set irregularly. As with other parts of the south and west ranges, this building has gone through a number of changes during the Middle Ages. Much of what can now be seen dates to the middle years of the thirteenth century, but this replaced an earlier building on the same site, which may have been largely of timber construction.

The refectory is entered from the cloister through a central doorway, but only one stone of the left side of the arch survives. Once inside, notice the square sockets for five pairs of vertical posts, set at evenly spaced intervals in the tops of the east and west walls.

These postholes supported the timber uprights for the roof of the building. Towards the far right corner, you will see the base of a fine spiral staircase, of which four steps still survive; note the fine carved dog-tooth decoration on the remains of the archway leading to the stairs. The architectural detail surviving here suggests a date for the construction of this refectory not long before the mid-thirteenth-century fire.

The staircase itself led up to a pulpit, from which one of the monks would have read to his brothers during meals. A finely carved stone head, inscribed with the name MORVS, was found during the excavations, and may once have flanked the reader's arch of the pulpit; this is one of the finest pieces of Cistercian sculpture known from Wales, and it has been suggested that this head might commemorate a major figure in the early church, such as St Maurus (died AD 584) or Rabanus Maurus (died AD 856). The internal arrangements of the refectory would have been much the same as in any other medieval great hall, with tables set parallel to the side walls and a high table at the south end. On the outer face of the two southern corners of the refectory are two large clasping buttresses, which helped spread the thrust of the roof.

The Kitchen ⬥15

The last structure in the south range was the abbey kitchen, situated where it could serve the refectories of both the choir monks and the lay brothers. It was probably linked to both by serving hatches set in the end walls. First constructed in the early thirteenth century, the kitchen has been rebuilt a number of times during the course of the Middle Ages. It is a rectangular room set parallel to the cloister. The walls again survive to a height of some 3 feet (1m) and are built of thinly coursed slates, incorporating some random rubble. It is entered from the cloister through a door in the left-hand side of its north wall. The lower part of the surviving door jamb bears a round moulding with a narrow fillet and is unlikely to be any earlier than the middle years of the thirteenth century. As in the refectory, there was a similar arrangement of sockets for timber posts in the surrounding walls. Similarly, excavations have suggested that the earliest phase may have been largely in timber, which was rebuilt in stone in the mid-thirteenth century.

Although many features discovered during archaeological excavations are no longer visible, the early thirteenth-century kitchen had an open hearth in the middle of the eastern half of the room. After the disastrous mid-thirteenth-century fire, the kitchen was rebuilt with a thin screen wall dividing it into two rooms. The building was again seriously damaged by fire in the early fifteenth century. When it was rebuilt, a large fireplace was inserted into the western end of the south wall and this can still be seen. Its sides are lined with moulded sandstone jambs and it has a large external chimney.

Above: The base of the spiral stairs in the refectory that led to the pulpit, from which a monk would read to the community during meals. The jambs are decorated with dog-tooth ornament.

Left: This carved head, one of the finest pieces of Welsh Cistercian sculpture, was found during the excavation of the refectory and may once have flanked the reader's pulpit. The figure is crowned with the name MORVS and it may represent St Maurus (d. 584) or the early medieval religious scholar and commentator Rabanus Maurus (d. 856) (National Museum of Wales).

The base of a large fireplace in the south wall of the abbey kitchen. The position of the kitchen allowed it to serve both the monks' refectory and the lay brothers' refectory in the west range, probably via serving hatches built into the walls.

The West Range

The west range was a two-storied block of buildings and was largely the domain of the lay brothers up until at least the mid-fourteenth century; thereafter, as the importance of the lay brothers declined, this part of the monastery would have been reorganized. In its original form, the ground floor was divided into four principal rooms, which are identified as a cellar, a passage, the lay brothers' refectory and a parlour or day room. The first floor would have been taken up by the lay brothers' dormitory, but no trace of this now remains. Most of the superstructure of the range was demolished by the construction of an eighteenth-century house. Parts of this range were first exposed in 1893, when oak timbers were recorded beneath some parts of the earliest walling, plus evidence for 'three or four distinct burnings'. Unfortunately, overenthusiastic clearance has removed any surviving evidence for the late medieval

Although only low walls now remain, the west range — in the foreground of this picture — was a two-storey block of buildings. It was largely the domain of the lay brothers, or conversi, *until their numbers declined in the later fourteenth century and the buildings were put to other uses.*

use of this range. In addition, attempts to partially reconstruct some of the structure, especially the west porch, make it difficult to be certain what is original, and what has been reconstructed.

Excavation in 1970 established that during the course of the Middle Ages, two projecting rooms had been built onto the outside of the west wall of the range; one of these structures was the lay brothers' latrine, which would have been served by a chute from the first-floor dormitory. No trace of these rooms is now visible.

The Lay Brothers' Refectory and the Cellarer's Office ◆16

The far southern end of the range was probably originally occupied by the lay brothers' refectory, but little of this is now visible. It would have been connected to the kitchen on the east by a serving

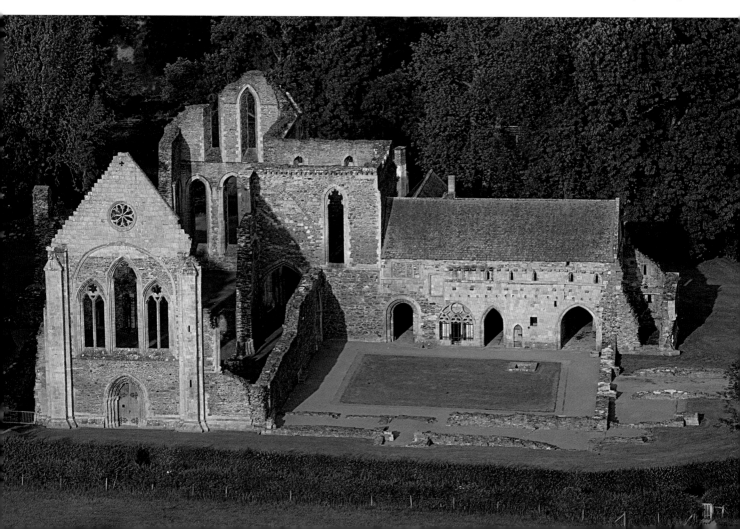

hatch. It was built in the early thirteenth century, but was demolished in the later Middle Ages, by which time the lay brothers had ceased to be an important element in the community. Only the footings of the north wall can now be seen.

By the later fourteenth century, the lay brothers' refectory had fallen out of use and was replaced by the cellarer's office. This is the small rectangular room that can now be seen in this position. It was used as an administrative office by the monk who looked after the abbey's financial affairs.

The Day Room or Parlour

Next there is a long rectangular room, the walls of which still stand to a height of 3.5 feet (1.08m). A stone-lined drain runs diagonally across the room and passes under the inner wall on its way to feed the monks' washing trough on the opposite side of the cloister. The room itself was probably the place where the lay brothers could relax and rest when they were not working.

Although nothing survives above ground, we know from excavations that the lay brothers' latrine was situated beyond the outer wall. Like the monks' latrine, it was a two-storied block, which would have been accessible from the dormitory on the first floor, but in this case it was a half-timbered structure. It was originally flushed by a stone drain, but had passed out of use by the later Middle Ages.

The Lay Brothers' Passage and the Porch 18

The passage was placed centrally in the western range and would originally have opened directly into the cloister. The interior, however, has been extensively disturbed by the construction of a new entrance into the cloister in 1889. This entailed the rebuilding of part of the east (inner) wall of the range, which now blocks the original entrance from the passage into the cloister. Part of the north wall of the passage still survives and incorporates the base of one side of a door. Although this has been reset in the nineteenth century, it probably marks an original entrance into the cellar to the north.

In the fourteenth century a stone porch was built onto the outer (west) side of this passage. This was heavily restored by the Victorians, who incorporated reused dressed stone, and it is now difficult to be certain how much is original.

The Cellar 19

The northern end of the west range, butting against the church, is a cellar. It is amongst the earliest surviving buildings at the abbey and, in part, its construction may have preceded that of the western end of the church. The evidence for this comes from the complex junction where the corner buttress at the western end of the south aisle meets the cellar.

Very few of the internal features of this cellar can now be seen. In the south-west corner, the base of a staircase appears to have been built onto the back of the north wall of the passage and this must have led up to the dormitory on the first floor. A doorway would originally have led into the south aisle of the church; although faint traces of the base of a door were suggested during the excavation, nothing is now visible. It is through this doorway that the lay brothers must have passed to attend their services. Finally, a stone-lined drain was found during excavations. This ran diagonally across the centre of the room and passed through a break in the east wall from where it presumably flowed across the cloister to the monks' washing trough, and the monks' latrine.

Originally, the lay brothers' refectory and day room occupied the southern half of the ground floor of the west range and the dormitory ran the entire length of the upper floor. After the refectory fell out of use in the late Middle Ages, it was replaced by the cellarer's office, the small rectangular building in the foreground of this view.

The cellarer was the Cistercian monastic official who oversaw the abbey's financial affairs and supervised its stocks of food, drink and fuel. In this early thirteenth-century manuscript illustration, a cellarer samples the contents of a cask while the keys symbolic of his office dangle from his fingers (© British Library Board, Sloane Ms. 2435, f. 44v).

Memorial Sculpture at the Abbey

Over twenty sculptured grave slabs, either whole or fragmentary, have been found within or near the church at Valle Crucis Abbey. A selection of the best of these has been gathered together and is on display in the dormitory.

Introduction

Monumental sculpture in north Wales was first introduced from England during the second quarter of the thirteenth century and from then until the conquest of Wales by King Edward I in 1283 it was almost entirely English in design. After the conquest, the Welsh stone carvers gradually moved away from the current English styles and developed their own attractive school of memorial sculpture in north Wales, and some of the finest examples of this work have survived at Valle Crucis. Important local families, who either founded or supported the various religious houses, chose to have their tombs marked by these memorial slabs. In some cases, it has been possible to piece together the identity of these individuals from the inscriptions, albeit often fragmentary, upon their graves.

The stones within the dormitory at Valle Crucis have been grouped together into distinctive monument types and are laid out in roughly chronological order.

Sepulchral Slab 1237–82

1   The mutilated fragment of a slab which has been trimmed down both sides for a later, secondary, use. The carving is well preserved and shows the lower part of a shaft, which was probably surmounted by a floriated cross. Stems, with bunches of fruit, branch downwards from the main shaft towards the

stiff-leaf foliage. The design of this slab is very similar to the carved lid of a stone coffin now preserved in Beaumaris church, which is almost certainly from the tomb of Princess Joan (d. 1237), the wife of Prince Llywelyn ab Iorwerth. Therefore, it seems possible that this fragment formed part of the tomb of the founder of Valle Crucis, Madog ap Gruffudd Maelor (d. 1236) of northern Powys (p. 9). The slab was found at an unrecorded location within the abbey about 1900.

Sepulchral Slabs 1282–1310

2   Fragment of the head of a slab with part of an inscription surrounding a panel decorated with unequal arches containing tracery in the Decorated style. This stone is very badly weathered. The surviving portion of the inscription reads:

✠ HIC ⫶ IACET ⫶ EV(A) …
Here lies Eva …
(About 1300)

3   Fragment of a small tapering slab with part of an inscription bordering decoration consisting of curving and interlacing stems and leaves. The surviving portion of the inscription reads:

… AIA ⫶ IN ⫶ PA(CE)
… soul in peace
(About 1300)

4   The side of a slab with part of an inscription bordering decoration consisting of curving and interlocking stems and leaves. The small portion of inscription reads:

TER
(About 1300)

5   The top corner of a slab with an inscription around its border and a panel decorated with leaves and curling stems. The stone is badly defaced. The surviving portion of the inscription reads:

✠ (HIC ⫶ I)ACET ⫶ DYDGU ⫶ F(ILIA) …
Here lies Dyddgu, daughter of …
(About 1300)

6   Fragments of a very badly weathered slab which has an inscription, placed within a border, surrounding a narrow band of decoration. This consists of the upper part of two animals with their heads back to back and their tails interlacing elaborately with two circles. The lower part of the panel has interlacing stems. The inscription reads:

✠ HIC ⫶ IACET(⫶)GWEIRCA (⫶ F)ILIA ⫶ OWENI ⫶ …
°PPICIETVR ⫶ …AME … E ⫶ ÅDÕ ⫶ ṀCĊ LẊXXX
Here lies Gweirca, daughter of Owain … (may God) have mercy … on her soul … A D 1290

This is the earliest dated slab in north Wales. Gweirca is probably a member of the family descended from the founder of the abbey, Madog ap Gruffudd Maelor, who was possibly her great-grandfather. The Madog mentioned on slab 12 would have been her cousin.

[16] This mutilated slab has been built in as part of the post-suppression chimney breast over the fireplace in the abbot's private chamber next to the dormitory. It has been trimmed and part of its lower end is missing. An inscription, placed in a border, surrounds an area of decoration consisting of a vine trail with large stylized leaves and bunches of grapes. This extends into the upper section of the slab where it branches out into an elaborate interlacing pattern. Towards the bottom of the stone, the stem is held in the jaws of an animal, part of whose foot can also be seen. The surviving portion of the inscription reads:

HIC IACET ⫶ MARVRVET ⫶ F(ILIA) …
Here lies Maruruet, daughter of …
(Early fourteenth century)

Expanded-Arm Crosses 1282–1320

7   A long narrow slab, carved in relief with an expanded-arm cross decorated with three ribs on the arms and shaft which overlap at the centre.
(Late thirteenth century)

8 A slab carved in relief with an expanded-arm cross, the shaft of which is incised with the outline of a sword. Between the point of the blade and the foot of the cross there is a simple pattern formed of two sets of lobes side by side, projecting inwards and downwards. The slab was discovered in about 1890 when fallen debris was being cleared from the north aisle of the church.
(Late thirteenth century)

9 A slab carved in incised outline and low relief with an expanded-arm cross. Between the arms there are four decorated circles and, on either side of the plain shaft, a spear and a sword. It was found covering the skeleton of a man in the early 1950s, while material was being cleared from outside the north aisle wall of the church.
(Late thirteenth century)

10 A slab which is broken in two and badly weathered. The head consists of an expanded-arm cross, the shaft of which extends down the length of the stone and divides into 'roots' at the foot. On one side of the shaft a sword is bordered by a zigzag pattern, which also appears above the cross at the head of the stone. On the other, there is a spear with a stem and leaf pattern between it and the edge of the stone. It was discovered in the cloister walk near the south door of the church in 1896. Nothing was found under the stone.
(Late thirteenth century)

Four-Circle Cross 1300–50

11 The upper part of a slab which has been badly defaced on one side by having been used for sharpening knives. The surviving carving is very worn. The design within the circular head consists of four open-ended circles interlacing with a central circle containing a four-petalled flower. Part of the inscription survives on one side of a plain narrow shaft:
✠ AWR : VO …
Awr foel (?)

This may be the monument of Awr ab Ieuaf, whose grandson's effigy is monument **14**.
(About 1300)

Heraldic Slabs

12 This slab and the grave beneath it were found in front of the high altar in the church. Recovered in 1956, it is perhaps the finest surviving monument of this period in north Wales, with the carving in almost perfect condition. A shield with a lion rampant and surrounded by an inscription is placed in the upper half of the slab. A sword lies diagonally behind the shield, while a spear is placed vertically up the full length of the slab. The remainder of the decoration consists of free designs of naturalistic foliage and bunches of fruit. The high quality of this workmanship is in marked contrast to the crudely executed lion on the shield. The inscription reads:
+ HIC IACET : MA /DOC' : FIL' : GRIFINI : DCI : VYCHAN :
Here lies Madog son of Gruffudd called Fychan

Madog ap Gruffudd (d. 1306), was the great-grandson of the founder of the abbey, and cousin of Gweirca mentioned on slab **6**. He was the great-grandfather of Owain Glyn Dŵr. Indeed Glyn Dŵr was able to claim that he was the sole surviving direct male descendant of one of the Welsh princely dynasties.

13 Fragments of one side of a large slab. A shield in the upper part of the slab has a lion rampant, and was originally surrounded by an inscription, part of which survives. A spear divides the lower half of the slab into two, and on either side of it are scenes from a hunt. On one side the front feet of a hound and hare in chase can be seen, while on the other a human head is blowing a hunting horn, and there are leaves and twining stems. It was found at the west end of the choir during excavations in 1851. The surviving portion of the inscription reads:
(✠HIC : IACET :). EDW(:FI)LIVꝶ : YO …
Here lies Edward son of Iorwerth
(Early fourteenth century)

Military Effigy 1282–1350

14 Fragments of a worn and mutilated slab with one of its top corners missing. One side has been trimmed away. A wide border containing an inscription ran round the entire slab, the upper part of which is carved in very deep false-relief with the head and shoulders of a knight together with part of his shield. The surviving portion of the inscription reads:
✠ HIC : IACET : YEVAF (:A)P : AD(DA … REQUIESCAT : IN : PAC)E : AMEN
Here lies Ieuaf ab Adda … may he rest in peace, Amen

This is generally taken to be the monument of Ieuaf ab Adda ab Awr ab Ieuaf, a powerful landowner in the nearby village of Trefor. If this is correct, then his grandfather, Awr, is the person commemorated on slab **11**. These fragments were found in the presbytery during excavations in 1851.
(Early fourteenth century)

Unclassified

15 A plain slab, the upper side of which is chamfered along its two long sides, with a fine incised line running from head to foot.

*The arms of Madog ap Gruffudd (d. 1306) from tomb slab **12**.*

The Pillar of Eliseg

Nancy Edwards BA, PhD, FSA

History

Valle Crucis (valley of the cross) takes its name from the remains of a tall ninth-century cross, which stands a short distance north of the ruins of the later Cistercian abbey. The surviving column bears a lengthy and elaborate, but now fragmentary, Latin inscription proclaiming the achievements and ancestry of the kings of Powys.

By the time that the Celtic scholar, Edward Lhuyd (d. 1709), visited the site in 1696 and copied the inscription, the monument was broken into several pieces. The upper part of the shaft, bearing the first half of the inscription, was re-erected in its original socket in 1779 — an act that is recorded in a framed Latin inscription on the reverse. The rest was lost. The original inscription, only partly legible in Lhuyd's day, is now so badly weathered that the carved area and some fragments of letters can only be distinguished in good light. We have to rely on Lhuyd for the text.

Before the shaft was re-erected, the mound upon which it stands was excavated. The only record of this was written long after the event and is difficult to interpret in detail, but a skeleton was found in or under the mound. It lay in a long cist or coffin formed of large blue stones. The large silver 'coin' said to have been found with the skeleton is a mystery, but it may have been a brooch or ornament buried with the corpse. The skull was removed and gilded for preservation, but was then replaced with the other bones. It has been suggested that this was the grave of Eliseg, a later eighth-century ruler of Powys, but this is unlikely because Christian burial without grave goods was the usual practice by this time and burial in churchyards was becoming more common. The mound is perhaps a Bronze Age or a Romano-British barrow, and the grave may also be of this date. Alternatively, the barrow may have been reused

for a 'long cist' grave in the fifth or sixth centuries AD; burials of this kind have been identified cut into earlier barrows elsewhere in Wales. The cross is located so as to command the valley and the height of the barrow would have given it additional prominence in the landscape.

The Pillar of Eliseg may be viewed from the roadside. Access is via a kissing gate and up a moderate slope over rough pasture.

Opposite: The Pillar of Eliseg is part of a memorial cross set up by Concenn (d. AD 854), the last early medieval king of Powys, to honour his great-grandfather, Eliseg. By the time the Celtic scholar, Edward Lhuyd (d. 1709), visited in 1696 and copied the lengthy inscription on the cross, it already lay in fragments on the ground. The surviving fragment, which bears the first half of the inscription, was re-erected in the original base block of the cross in 1779, but the other pieces have been lost.

Edward Lhuyd's late seventeenth-century transcription of the text inscribed on the Pillar of Eliseg. As the incomplete lines demonstrate, much of the inscription was already illegible by this time. After three more centuries of weathering, it is now difficult to identify even fragments of letters on the shaft (Archives and Special Collections, Bangor University, Mss Penrhos V, 872; reproduced by kind permission of Lord Stanley of Alderney).

The Pillar of Eliseg is missing not only its lower portion, but also the carved cross-head that would originally have surmounted the shaft. Concenn's memorial cross was of a type well known in those parts of the north-west Midlands of England encompassed within the Anglo-Saxon kingdom of Mercia. The sculptured cross-shaft at Clulow, Cheshire, shown here, is a good example of the type, although it, too, is missing its cross-head. (There is no public right of way to the Clulow Cross.)

Apart from the Pillar of Eliseg, the cross-shaft in the churchyard at Corwen (Denbighshire) is the only known Welsh example of the type of cross familiar in the north-west Midlands.

Description

The Pillar of Eliseg now stands some 8 feet (2.41m) high, but its lower part is missing, the broken lower end having been inserted into the socket. In addition, there would originally have been a separate upper stone, ending in a carved cross-head. Its original height may have been close to 20 feet (6.1m). The custom of erecting tall sculptured crosses may have spread to Wales from parts of England and Ireland where they were already in use. The Pillar of Eliseg, before its mutilation, was a type of cross well known in parts of the English north-west Midlands, in the old kingdom of Mercia. The cross-shaft at Clulow, Cheshire, is a good example. The only similar cross-shaft in Wales stands in the churchyard at Corwen, about 10 miles (16km) to the west.

The lower part of the shaft is rounded, though somewhat squarish in section. The original inscription is cut on one of the rounded faces. It stands in its original rectangular base block, which now rests on a stone-rubble plinth. At a height of just under 6 feet (1.8m) there is a round collar, above which the shaft becomes square. The transition from round to square is marked by a curved roll moulding on each face, giving the surviving upper part the appearance of the capital of a column. The form may have been derived from wooden crosses where the lower part of the circular trunk was left intact, with the upper part shaved off into four faces. Roman columns are also likely to have been influential.

The Inscription

Originally, the Latin inscription was in at least thirty-one lines of Insular script. This was a type of writing developed in the monasteries of seventh-century Britain and Ireland for books of the Scriptures and other texts, as well as for inscriptions on stone. It remained in use for many centuries thereafter.

Each line of the inscription consisted of a little under thirty letters and the text was divided into at least nine phrases, each beginning with an initial cross, though not necessarily on a new line. Not all of it can now be read from Lhuyd's transcription and the following translation is necessarily tentative and incomplete; reconstructed parts are shown in brackets:

1   + Concenn son of Cattell, Cattell son of Brohcmail, Brohcmail son of Eliseg, Eliseg son of Guoilauc.

2   + Concenn therefore, the great-grandson of Eliseg, erected this stone in honour of his great-grandfather, Eliseg.

3   + It was Eliseg who (united) the inheritance of Pouos … through force …from the power of the English … (possessions with his sword by fire).

4   (+) Whosoever shall read out loud this hand-inscribed (stone), may he give a blessing (on the soul of) Eliseg.

5   + It is Concenn … with his hand … his own kingdom of Pouos … and which … the mountain.

6   … monarchy … Maximus of Britain … Pascent …Maun Annan …

7   Britu moreover was the son of Guarthi(girn), whom Germanus blessed, whom Sevira bore. (She was) the daughter of Maximus…, who killed the king of the Romans.

8   + Conmarch painted this writing at the command of his king, Concenn.

9   + The blessing of the Lord upon Concenn and likewise upon all of his household and upon all the land of Pouos until (the Day of Judgement).

The cross was set up by Concenn (Cyngen in modern Welsh), last of the early medieval kings of Powys. The death of his father, Catell (Cadell in modern Welsh), is recorded in the tenth-century chronicles known as the *Annales Cambriae* under the year AD 808. Concenn died in old age on a pilgrimage to Rome in AD 854 and therefore the monument can be dated to approximately the first half of the ninth century.

The inscription is of great significance as a historical document that can shed light on the history of the early medieval kingdom of Powys, particularly in the later eighth and first half of the ninth centuries. It was also in its time an important piece of public propaganda. It begins by establishing the genealogical link between Concenn and his great-grandfather, Eliseg, in whose honour he set up the cross [1, 2]. The inscription then proclaims Eliseg's success in the struggle against the English [3]. Eliseg would have been a contemporary of King Offa of Mercia who reigned between AD 757 and 796. English raids into Wales and other hostilities during Offa's reign are recorded in the *Annales Cambriae*. It has also been

suggested that the Mercians built Offa's Dyke as a defensive frontier between the kingdom of Powys, which had once stretched further east, and the kingdom of Mercia. The next phrase [4] is a standard commemorative formula, which also indicates that the inscription was intended to be read out loud to all those who could not read it for themselves. The following lines are fragmentary, but what survives suggests that the purpose of this phrase [5] was to praise Concenn's deeds as ruler of Powys in a way similar to those of Eliseg.

The following two phrases (only a few words in [6] can be read) take us back to the origins of the kingdom of Powys at the end of the Roman period. They appear to record the descent of the rulers of Powys from Britu (Brydw in modern Welsh), the son of Guarthigirn (Gwrtheyrn in modern Welsh, also known as Vortigern) and grandson of the Roman emperor, Magnus Maximus. Maximus, known as 'Macsen Wledig' (Macsen the Ruler) in later Welsh tradition, was a Spanish-born general who seized power in Britain in AD 383 and invaded Gaul. He slew the Emperor Gratian (AD 367–83), but was himself overthrown and executed in AD 388. It was normal for an early Welsh dynasty to legitimize its rule by claiming descent from a Roman emperor or a similarly heroic ancestor figure. Guarthigirn was reputedly the shadowy fifth-century

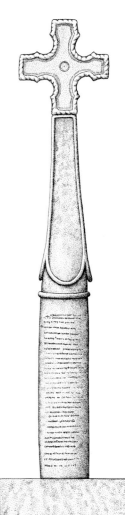

Above: An artist's impression of the Pillar of Eliseg in its original state, when its height may have been close to 20 feet (6.1m) (Howard Mason).

Left: This fifteenth-century manuscript illustration of a king may represent the Roman imperial claimant, Magnus Maximus (d. AD 388) — the Macsen Wledig of later Welsh tradition. The fragmentary inscription on the Pillar of Eliseg suggests that Concenn claimed descent from Magnus Maximus (National Library of Wales, Ms. 17520A, f. 3).

In this 1797 pen and wash drawing by Thomas Rowlandson (d. 1827), a party of tourists listen attentively as a guide points to some feature of the Pillar of Eliseg (National Library of Wales, PD9363).

'proud tyrant' whose memory was execrated for inviting Anglo-Saxon mercenaries into Britain. His later rebellion led to the foundation of the kingdom of Kent. St Germanus (Garmon in modern Welsh) may be identified as a local saint associated with the kingdom of Powys.

Unusually, the penultimate phrase [8] tells us the name of the man, Conmarch, who probably composed the inscription at the behest of his patron, Concenn. The use of the specialized Latin term for 'writing' (*chirografum*) implies a 'charter' and thus a title deed for the dynasty, which draws attention to the legal formality of the whole inscription. It also suggests that the function of the cross and its inscription was to serve as a permanent and very visible sign of the possession of land and proof of ownership by the rulers of Powys, which was held in perpetuity with God's blessing [9].

Further Reading

Valle Crucis Abbey

L. A. S. Butler, 'Valle Crucis Abbey: An Excavation in 1970', *Archaeologia Cambrensis* **125** (1976), 80–126.

H. Hughes, 'Valle Crucis Abbey', *Archaeologia Cambrensis*, series 5, **11** (1894), 169–85, 257–75; **12** (1895), 5–17.

H. Hughes, 'Valle Crucis Abbey', *Archaeologia Cambrensis* **90** (1935), 333–43.

D. Pratt, *The Dissolution of Valle Crucis Abbey*, Dragon Local History Series 1 (second revised edition, Wrexham 1997).

G. V. Price, *Valle Crucis Abbey* (Liverpool 1952).

C. A. R. Radford, *Valle Crucis Abbey* (HMSO, London 1953).

The Cistercians

R. A. Donkin, *The Cistercians: Studies in the Geography of Medieval England and Wales* (Toronto 1978).

Peter Fergusson, *Architecture of Solitude: Cistercian Abbeys in Twelfth-Century England* (Princeton 1984).

Christopher Norton and David Park, editors, *Cistercian Art and Architecture in the British Isles* (Cambridge 1986).

David Robinson (editor), *The Cistercian Abbeys of Britain: Far From the Concourse of Men* (London 1998).

David M. Robinson, *The Cistercians in Wales: Architecture and Archaeology 1130–1540*, Reports of the Research Committee of the Society of Antiquaries of London 73 (London 2006).

D. H. Williams, *Atlas of Cistercian Lands in Wales* (Cardiff 1990).

David H. Williams, *The Welsh Cistercians*, new edition (Leominster 2001).

Monastic History and Buildings

Mick Aston, *Monasteries in the Landscape* (Stroud 2002).

Janet Burton, *Monastic and Religious Orders in Britain 1000–1300* (Cambridge 1994).

Glyn Coppack, *Abbeys and Priories* (London 1990).

R. R. Davies, *Conquest, Coexistence, and Change: Wales 1063–1415* (Oxford 1987); reprinted in paperback as *The Age of Conquest: Wales 1063–1415* (Oxford 1991).

J. P. Greene, *Medieval Monasteries* (Leicester 1992).

D. Knowles and R. N. Hadcock, *Medieval Religious Houses: England and Wales*, 2nd edition (London 1971).

C. H. Lawrence, *Medieval Monastic Life in Western Europe in the Middle Ages*, third edition (Harlow 2001).

C. Platt, *The Abbeys and Priories of Medieval England* (London 1984).

Monumental Sculpture and the Pillar of Eliseg

J. Romilly Allen, 'Eliseg's Pillar', *Archaeologia Cambrensis*, series 5, **11** (1894), 220–23.

D. N. Dumville, 'Sub-Roman Britain: History and Legend', *History*, new series, **62** (1977), 173–92.

C. A. Gresham, *Medieval Stone Carving in North Wales* (Cardiff 1968).

R. A. S. Macalister, *Corpus Inscriptionum Insularum Celticarum*, Vol. II (Dublin, 1949), no. 1000.

V. E. Nash-Williams, *Early Christian Monuments of Wales* (Cardiff 1950).

J. Rhys, 'All around the Wrekin', *Y Cymmrodor* **21** (1908), 1–62.